D1413608

Have Breakfast with Us... Again

Recipes & Relaxation

from Wisconsin Bed and Breakfast Homes
and Historic Inns Association

Amherst Press
a division of Palmer Publications, Inc.
Amherst, Wisconsin

Copyright © 1995 Amherst Press

First edition 1995
Third edition 1997

All rights reserved. Reproduction in whole or in part of any portion in any form without permission of publisher is prohibited.

Amherst Press
A Division of Palmer Publications, Inc.
318 N. Main Street
Amherst, Wisconsin 54406

Library of Congress Cataloging in Publication Data

Wisconsin Bed and Breakfast Homes and Historic Inns Association.
      Have breakfast with us—again: recipes & relaxation/from Wisconsin
    Bed and Breakfast Homes and Historic Inns Association. —
    1st ed.
       p. cm.
       Includes index.
       ISBN 0-942495-44-6
       1. Breakfasts. 2. Bed and breakfast accommodations—Wisconsin—
Directories. I. Title.
TX733.W57   1995
647.94775'03—dc20   95-8849
                                              CIP

Designed and marketed by Amherst Press.
Printed in the United States of America by Palmer Publications, Inc.

Contents

Acknowledgments

Thank you to Terry Wulf and the staff
of The Inn at Cedar Crossing,
photographer Ric Genthe of Ric Genthe & Associates,
and watercolor artist Kathleen Parr McKenna
for their contributions to the book's cover.

Thank you also to the cookbook committee
of the Wisconsin Bed & Breakfast Homes
& Historic Inns Association and all the
participating members.

Participating Inns

Bayfield

Montreal

Barnes

Hayward

Eagle River   Florence
                  Spread Eagle

                  Crandon

Ogema

Osceola   Chetek   Sister Bay
                                                     Ephrain
Hudson   Fish Creek
Hammond   Menomonie   Sturgeon Bay
River Falls

                                                     Merrill

                                                     DePere

Maiden Rock   Stevens Point   Iola
          Wisconsin Rapids   Waupaca
Pepin   Two Rivers
               Plainfield   Manitowoc
                              Wild Rose

Sparta   Green Lake

               Endeavor   Plymouth
Lake Delton   Wisconsin Dells   Waupun
La Farge   Portage   Juneau
    Reedsburg Baraboo Poynette
Richland Center   Lodi   Port Washington
          Plain   Cedarburg
Spring Green   Watertown
Cross Plains Middleton Lake Mills   Menomonee Falls

                         Fort Atkinson
          Edgerton   Whitewater

                                     Burlington
          Albany   Elkhorn
                         Delavan
          Monroe   Lake Geneva

City Guide to Participating Inns

Albany Guest House

405 South Mill Street, Albany, WI 53502
608-862-3636

Hosts: Bob and Sally Braem

Take our brick walk from the flower-surrounded parking area to the restored three-story block home with refinished wood floors, supporting king- and queen-size beds and private baths. Light the wood in the Master Bedroom fireplace or swing on the front porch. Stroll the two-acre garden-filled yard, or bike the nearby Sugar River Trail. Rent a canoe or visit nearby Swiss communities. Guests are served generous, healthy breakfasts with homemade syrups, breads, and jellies.

Rates at the Albany Guest House range from $55–$68.
Rates include a full breakfast.

Banana Whole Grain Waffles

This super-nutritious entree is very satisfying and delicious;
guests appreciate our concern for their health.
Leftovers can be toasted (in halves) and eaten with low-fat
cottage cheese on top, then covered with fruit
or fruit sauce for a complete lunch.

serves 4-5

1/2	cup flour	1	teaspoon salt
3/4	cup whole wheat flour	3	teaspoons baking powder
1/2	cup wheat germ	1	teaspoon cinnamon
1/4	cup cornmeal	2	eggs, separated
1/4	cup wheat bran	1	banana, mashed
2	tablespoons oat bran	1 1/2	cups skim milk
2	tablespoons brown sugar	2	tablespoons canola oil

Spray waffle iron with cooking spray if necessary; then preheat.

Stir together flours, wheat germ, cornmeal, wheat bran, oat bran, brown sugar, salt, baking powder, and cinnamon in a large bowl. In a small bowl, whisk together egg yolks, mashed banana, milk, and oil. Add to dry ingredients, blending thoroughly. Whip egg whites until stiff and fold into batter.

Ladle batter into center of preheated waffle iron. Bake, allowing waffle to steam, until golden brown, 3-5 minutes. Serve with fruit syrups, sauces, fresh fruit, or maple syrup.

Oak Hill Manor

401 East Main Street, Albany, WI 53502
608-862-1400

Hosts: Lee and Mary DeWolf

At Oak Hill Manor, seated on an acre of gardens, summer brings a bounty of fruits and vegetables: strawberries, blackberries, and grapes for jam and fresh spinach for our Eggs Florentine. Breakfast is a grand, gourmet affair served on china with crystal and silver service.

Summer days start with early morning coffee on the porch overlooking the fountain in the flower gardens, and winter breakfast is served in front of the fire. Take an afternoon break in the gazebo with a glass of lemonade and a selection of fine Green County cheeses.

Our home is decorated and furnished as it would have been at the turn of the century. The four spacious guest rooms are air-conditioned, and all have private baths.

Rates at the Oak Hill Manor are $60.
Rates include a full breakfast.

Eggs Florentine

*You'll find this "one pan" breakfast
simple to make but oh so elegant to serve.
A perfect vegetarian alternative to Eggs Benedict.*

serves 6

6 eggs
6 tomato slices, 1/2-inch thick
   Parmesan cheese, grated
6 slices bread, toasted
   Bacon, cooked and crumbled,
     optional

Sauce:
1/4 cup butter
1/4 cup flour
1/2 teaspoon salt
1/2 teaspoon hot pepper sauce
2 cups milk
1 pound fresh spinach, washed and
     coarsely chopped or 1 10-ounce
     package frozen spinach, thawed
     and drained

To prepare sauce, make a roux with butter, flour, salt, and hot sauce in a heavy 10-inch skillet with a tight-fitting lid. Cook 2 minutes, stirring constantly. Slowly stir in milk and heat until thickened. Add spinach and bring sauce to a boil.

Carefully break eggs, one at a time, into spinach sauce. Cover skillet and cook over low heat 7-9 minutes.

Meanwhile, sprinkle tomato slices with cheese and broil until cheese is bubbly and tomatoes are heated through.

Place one tomato slice on each toast slice and, with a large spoon, remove each egg and place on tomato slices. Spoon additional sauce over top, sprinkle with bacon, and serve immediately.

Pinehaven Bed & Breakfast

E13083 Highway 33, Baraboo, WI 53913
608-356-3489

Hosts: Lyle and Marge Getschman

At Pinehaven we are very grateful for our scenic location and love to share it with our guests. They enjoy a quiet, serene country setting with a small spring-fed lake, a wonderful view of the Baraboo bluffs in all seasons, relaxing in our gazebo, screened porch or decks, and watching the hummingbirds. Our Belgian draft horses and farm tours are an added attraction as is the nearby popular tourist area.

We have four guest rooms with private baths, air conditioning, and queen-size or twin beds. Ask about our private guest house.

Rates at the Pinehaven Bed & Breakfast range from $65-$95.
Rates include a full breakfast.

Blueberry Coffee Cake

serves 10-12

		Topping:	
2	cups flour	1/2	cup sugar
3/4	cup sugar	1/3	cup flour
2 1/2	teaspoons baking powder	1	teaspoon cinnamon
1/4	teaspoon salt	1/4	cup butter, melted
1/4	cup butter		
1/4	cup milk	Icing:	
1/2	cup sour cream	1/2	cup powdered sugar
1	egg		Water
2	cups fresh blueberries		

Preheat oven to 375 degrees. Grease 9-inch springform pan with 3-inch sides.

In a large bowl, blend together flour, sugar, baking powder, and salt. Cut in butter. Add milk, sour cream, and egg. Beat with spoon 30 seconds and fold in blueberries. Spread batter carefully into pan.

Combine sugar, flour, cinnamon, and butter to make topping and sprinkle over batter.

Bake 45-50 minutes. Combine powdered sugar and enough water for icing with a drizzling consistency. Drizzle over cake while cake is still warm.

Sunset Resort Bed & Breakfast Lodge

HCR61 Box 6325, Barnes, WI 54873
715-795-2449, 1-800-38-SUNSET

Hosts: Cher and Dan TePoel

Our 1943 cedar lodge on the Eau Claire Lake Chain is nestled among tall pines and giant oaks and offers a year-round picturesque view and quiet solitude. Start your day with a hearty country breakfast served fireside in the dining room.

We have everything you need to enjoy a relaxing escape to the beautiful north woods for a hideaway-getaway. Picnic on an island, boat or canoe scenic waterways, or enjoy a cozy fire by a stone fireplace.

Sunset Resort is a comfy, old-fashioned, country sort of place with a touch of today. Your hosts offer an atmosphere that's warm and friendly in a quiet relaxed country setting.

Rates at the Sunset Resort Bed & Breakfast Lodge range from $55–$65. Rates include a full breakfast.

12

Pannekuechen (Dutch)

Pannekuechen rises like a giant cream puff.
It is very easy and quick to make and can be served
with any fruit, sour cream, whipped cream,
or crumbled bacon. Use your imagination.
You will be sharing this recipe a lot with guests.

serves 8

1/2	cup butter
6	eggs
1	cup flour
1	cup milk
1/2	teaspoon salt

Topping Suggestions:
Sour cream
Fresh strawberry jam

Place butter in 9x13-inch glass baking dish. Place pan in oven at 450 degrees until melted. Do not preheat oven!

While butter is melting, beat eggs in blender or with electric mixer. Add flour, milk, and salt; mix well.

When batter is smooth, take baking dish out of oven and pour mixture over butter. Return to oven to bake for 20 minutes. DO NOT OPEN OVEN WHILE BAKING!

Serve with sour cream and fresh strawberry jam. Syrup is optional.

The Old Rittenhouse Inn

301 Rittenhouse Avenue, P.O. Box 584, Bayfield, WI 54814
715-779-5111

Hosts: Jerry and Mary Phillips

Situated on a tree-covered hillside in picturesque Bayfield, Wisconsin, The Old Rittenhouse Inn offers visitors feasts for the eyes and the soul, with spectacular views of Lake Superior and the Apostle Islands, as well as for the taste buds.

Guest rooms all offer wood-burning fireplaces, laid ready-to-light, as well as private baths. All are furnished and decorated in Victorian style, as are the three dining rooms on the main floor of the Inn.

Innkeepers Mary and Jerry Phillips feature the best and freshest of local produce and "wild things," from fiddlehead ferns to fresh Lake Superior trout, in imaginative dishes offered at breakfast, Sunday brunch, and dinnertime.

A five-course gourmet dinner is served each evening through the summer and early fall. The dining room is open to the public.

Rates at The Old Rittenhouse Inn range from $99–$189.
Rates include a continental breakfast; a full breakfast is also available.

Wild Rice Pancakes

serves 6-8

4	cups buttermilk	2	tablespoons sugar
3/4	cup vegetable oil	1 1/2	teaspoons salt
1	cup flour	4	eggs
1/2	cup cake flour	2	cups cooked wild rice
1	teaspoon baking powder	1/2	cup sour cream
1	teaspoon baking soda	1/4	cup powdered sugar

Mix buttermilk and oil in large bowl. Combine flours, baking powder, baking soda, sugar, and salt in another bowl. Gradually add dry mixture to buttermilk mixture. Mix well. Add eggs to batter, stirring until well combined. Let batter rest 30 minutes.

Spoon batter onto hot griddle using about a half cup for each cake. Sprinkle cooked wild rice onto cakes to your liking. Flip cakes when bubbles in the batter open up. Remove pancakes to warmed plates, top with a dollop of sour cream, dust with powdered sugar, and serve with real maple syrup.

Thimbleberry Inn Bed & Breakfast

15021 Pageant Road, P.O. Box 1007, Bayfield, WI 54814
715-779-5757

Hosts: Sharon and Craig Locey

*T*his brand new contemporary home features 375 feet of Lake
Superior frontage and enjoys viewing five of the Apostle
Islands! The three guest rooms each have a private entrance,
private bath, and a real working fireplace. Guests enjoy freshly-
brewed gourmet coffee from Madeline Island and homemade muffins
delivered to their room in Longaberger baskets a half hour prior to a
full gourmet breakfast. Breakfast is served on the spacious deck
(weather permitting) or in the dining area overlooking the islands.

Thimbleberry Inn is located just south of Schooner Bay. Its lovely
wooded setting offers you a quiet secluded getaway. You can walk
among the trees on our 40 acres or along the lake or just relax in your
own outdoor Adirondack love seats and enjoy the restful sound of the
waves lapping against the shore. You may be fortunate enough to see
one of several eagles that soar along our lake shore.

Rates at the Thimbleberry Inn Bed & Breakfast range from $75–$115.
Rates include a full breakfast.

Craisin Yogurt Muffins

These muffins have been a favorite of our guests since we opened on May 28, 1993. They are very easy to prepare and the batter keeps well in the refrigerator for several days if you want to double the recipe. The yogurt makes for a very moist and tender muffin.

makes 12 muffins

1	cup oatmeal	3/4	teaspoon salt
1	cup vanilla yogurt	1/2	teaspoon baking soda
1/2	cup vegetable oil	1	teaspoon baking powder
3/4	cup brown sugar	1/2	cup craisins
1	egg		(dried cranberries)
1	cup flour		Powdered sugar

In large bowl, soak oatmeal in yogurt for 5 minutes. Add oil, sugar, and egg and beat well.

In medium bowl, sift together flour, salt, baking soda, and baking powder. Add to ingredients in large bowl. Fold in craisins.

Fill greased muffin tins and bake at 400 degrees for 20 minutes. Sprinkle with powdered sugar before serving.

Hillcrest Inn and Carriage House

540 Storle Avenue, Burlington, WI 53105
414-763-4706

Hosts: Dick and Karen Granholm

A Recipe for Serenity and Romance:

Combine a stately Edwardian mansion with exquisite decor and lovely antiques.

Blend in a charming carriage house with fireplaces and double whirlpools.

Sprinkle four acres with English flower gardens and winding walking paths.

Mix two expansive porches with a magnificent view, and serve with a beautiful sunset.

Rates at the Hillcrest Inn range from $60–$150.
Rates include a full breakfast.

Karen's Quick and Easy Blueberry Muffins

*These muffins can be made
with any fresh or frozen berries: cherries, cranberries, etc.
They freeze well and can be heated (after freezing)
for 10 minutes at 350 degrees to taste like freshly-baked.*

makes 16 muffins

2^1/$_2$	cups biscuit mix
1	cup brown sugar, loosely packed
^{1}/$_2$	cup butter, melted
^{1}/$_4$	cup milk
2	eggs
^{1}/$_4$	cup applesauce
1	cup blueberries, fresh or frozen

Topping:
^{1}/$_4$	cup white sugar
1	teaspoon cinnamon

In medium bowl, stir together biscuit mix and brown sugar. Add butter, milk, eggs, and applesauce. Stir until just mixed; batter will be lumpy. Carefully fold in blueberries. Drop by spoonfuls into paper-lined muffin tins. In small bowl, combine sugar and cinnamon for topping. Sprinkle each muffin with approximately 1 teaspoon of topping.

Bake in 375-degree oven for 15 minutes, or until wooden pick inserted in center comes out clean.

Stagecoach Inn

W61 N520 Washington Avenue, Cedarburg, WI 53012
414-375-0208

Hosts: Liz and Brook Brown; Claudia Connor

The Stagecoach Inn is a historically restored 1853 stone building in downtown Cedarburg listed on the National Register. Twelve rooms are comfortably furnished with antiques, handstenciled walls, private baths, and central air. The suites feature luxurious oversized whirlpools. A hearty continental breakfast is served in the pub, which becomes the "gathering room" in the evening. Treat yourself to handmade chocolates from Beernsten's candy store before exploring Cedarburg's numerous antique and gift shops, art studios, beautiful parks, and seasonal festivals. "A Little Country Inn in the City."

Rates at the Stagecoach Inn range from $70–$105.
Rates include a continental breakfast.

Apple-Cinnamon French Toast

The apple cider syrup fills the kitchen with a
wonderful aroma that makes your guests believe
that you've been up all night baking just for them!

serves 6

		Apple Cider Syrup:	
8	eggs	1	cup sugar
1	cup milk		Dash cinnamon
	Dash salt	3	tablespoons cornstarch
12	cinnamon croissants, sliced	2	cups apple cider
	in half lengthwise or 1 loaf	1	tablespoon lemon juice
	cinnamon swirl bread,	4	tablespoons margarine
	sliced 3/4-thick		

In medium bowl, beat together eggs, milk, and salt. Soak croissants or bread slices in mixture for 10 minutes.

Meanwhile prepare syrup. Mix together sugar, cinnamon, and cornstarch in 2-quart saucepan. Add cider and lemon juice. Cook over medium heat until mixture thickens, stirring often. Remove from heat and stir in margarine. (Syrup can be prepared ahead and re-heated.)

On a hot griddle, fry egg-soaked bread until golden brown on each side. Serve with hot Apple Cider Syrup. For a "treat," serve with a scoop of vanilla ice cream on top of French toast.

Trails End Bed & Breakfast

641 Ten Mile Lake Drive, Chetek, WI 54728
715-924-2641

Hosts: Richard and Bonnie Flood

Come and join us in our modern three-level log lodge. We are on a privately owned island amid a chain of six lakes. We named the island Trails End, but as one editorial said, we should have called it "Fantasy Island."

If you are dreaming of a peaceful, quiet retreat where you can kick back and relax and let the rest of the world go by, this is the place. Maybe you want a little more action. There is fishing, boating, snowmobiling, cross-country skiing, biking, hiking, golfing, and of course, shopping.

Whether you stay in the Romantic, Indian, or Western room, our goal is to make you feel as though you have been to "Fantasy Island."

Rates at the Trails End Bed & Breakfast range from $80–$95.
Rates include a full breakfast.

Cinnamon Coffee Cake

*I received this recipe from a very special neighbor,
and it has turned out to be everyone's favorite.
Moist and scrumptiously delicious.*

serves 8

1	15-19-ounce package yellow cake mix	$^1/_2$	cup brown sugar
1	5.1-ounce package vanilla instant pudding	2	teaspoons cinnamon
$^3/_4$	cup oil	2	cups chopped walnuts
$^3/_4$	cup water		Frosting:
4	eggs	1	cup powdered sugar
1	teaspoon vanilla extract	1	teaspoon vanilla extract
2	teaspoons butter	2	teaspoons butter
			Cream or milk

In large mixing bowl, combine cake mix, pudding mix, oil, water, eggs, vanilla, and butter. Mix at high speed for 8 minutes. In a small bowl, combine brown sugar and cinnamon. Sprinkle chopped walnuts on bottom of greased 9x13-inch baking pan.

Over walnuts, layer half of brown sugar mixture, half of batter, remaining brown sugar mixture, and remaining batter. Using a knife, swirl ingredients in pan for a marble effect.

Bake at 350 degrees for 50-55 minutes.

To make frosting, combine powdered sugar, vanilla, butter, and enough cream to achieve spreading consistency. Spread over cake while still warm, but not hot.

Courthouse Square Bed & Breakfast

210 East Polk Street, Crandon, WI 54520
715-478-2549

Hosts: Les and Bess Aho

The serene peace, quiet, and natural beauty of the setting is frequently commented on by guests. Fragrant flower and herb gardens are found everywhere, and benches are placed throughout so you can enjoy the flowers and birds at the many feeders. Take a cup of coffee or a glass of iced tea and stroll down the hill through the forget-me-nots to the pastoral lake and enjoy the ducks and herons.

This turn-of-the-century home is a mecca of collections from advertising silhouettes to checkerboards to Fiesta ware that the morning candlelit breakfasts feature.

Guests enjoy the recreational facilities of the Nicolet National Forest, two local train rides, and nearby casinos (we offer a package) but also have the option of relaxing and enjoying the simple pleasure of a small town. The Rhinelander Daily News wrote, "Traditional hospitality is emphasized at Courthouse Square B & B and it's evident from the moment you enter this delightful home where tranquility and peace abounds. You will no doubt smell something delicious baking in Bess' kitchen as gourmet cooking is one of her specialties."

Rates at the Courthouse Square Bed & Breakfast range from $50-$60.
Rates include a full breakfast.

Orange Raisin Scones with Orange Butter

Scones are a great alternative to muffins for breakfast. These are particularly popular, and the orange butter enhances the flavor of the scones.

makes 8-12 scones

1³/₄	cups flour	Orange Butter:
3	tablespoons sugar	¹/₂ cup butter, softened
2¹/₂	teaspoons baking powder	2 tablespoons orange
2	teaspoons grated orange peel	marmalade
¹/₃	cup butter	
¹/₂	cup golden raisins	
2	eggs	
4-6	tablespoons half-and-half	

Preheat oven to 400 degrees. In medium bowl, combine flour, sugar, baking powder, and orange peel. Cut in butter until crumbly. Stir in raisins, 1 egg, lightly beaten, and enough half-and-half to just moisten mixture.

Turn dough onto lightly floured surface; knead lightly 10 times. Roll into 9-inch circle. Cut into 8-12 wedges. Place on cookie sheet 1 inch apart. Brush with remaining egg, beaten. Bake 10-12 minutes or until golden brown. Immediately remove from cookie sheet.

Make Orange Butter by mixing together butter and marmalade until combined. Serve with warm scones.

The Past & Present Inn & Dining Room

2034 Main Street, Cross Plains, WI 53528
608-798-4441

Hosts: Ken and Joyce Niesen

We invite you to join us at The Past & Present Inn, located in a peaceful valley, just nine beautiful miles from Madison, on Highway 14. We opened The Past & Present Gift Shop in November 1984, added the Dining Room in April 1987 and now announce the opening of the Bed and Breakfast Suites. Our ancestors helped settle the Cross Plains/Pine Bluff area, and we live just minutes away. Gracious service to our guests is top priority as we strive for exemplary standards in every detail at the Inn. We know you will enjoy a visit with us and hope to see you soon.

Rates at The Past & Present Inn range from $75–$150.
Rates include a full breakfast in our Dining Room restaurant.

Apple Filled Oven French Toast

Something hot and delicious to enjoy on a cold, snowy,
winter Wisconsin morning. Our stuffed French toast
is prepared the night before. In the morning
just pop it into the oven. Easy and scrumptious!

serves 8-10

1	loaf (12 ounces) French bread, cut in 1-inch slices	Topping:
1	21-ounce can apple filling	1/2 cup butter, softened
8	large eggs	1 cup brown sugar
2	cups milk	2 tablespoons dark corn syrup
2	cups half-and-half	1 cup coarsely chopped pecans, walnuts, or hickory nuts
2	teaspoons vanilla extract	
1/2	teaspoon nutmeg	
1/2	teaspoon cinnamon	

Heavily butter a 9x13-inch baking pan. Place one layer of bread slices in prepared pan. Spread apple filling over layer of bread. Place a layer of bread on top of apple filling. Set aside.

In blender, mix eggs, milk, half-and-half, vanilla, nutmeg, and cinnamon. Pour mixture over bread slices. Refrigerate covered, overnight.

Just before baking, make topping by combining butter, brown sugar, corn syrup, and nuts. Spread topping over toast; bake at 350 degrees for 50 minutes until puffed and golden.

The Allyn Mansion Inn, Ltd.

511 East Walworth Avenue, Delavan, WI 53115
414-728-9090

Hosts: Joe Johnson and Ron Markwell

The Allyn Mansion, located in the lakes area of southeastern Wisconsin, has been nationally recognized as one of the finest restoration efforts in the country. As a result of its renaissance under current owners Joe Johnson and Ron Markwell, it was the recipient of the National Trust's Great American Home Awards Grand Prize. After years of use and abuse as a nursing home and later a furniture store, Joe and Ron bought the derelict jewel in 1984 and have subsequently restored the grand old matriarch to her original glory, furnishing the interior with their notable collections of Victoriana. A must for the "traditional" B & B'er.

Rates at The Allyn Mansion Inn range from $50-$90.
Rates include a full breakfast.

Allyn Mansion Fried Apples

This simple dish always evokes memories of my childhood, growing up in the Ozarks of Southern Missouri. Fried apples were standard early-fall fare in our home. Served at breakfast, with ham from the smokehouse, red-eyed gravy, eggs, and hot biscuits, or later for dinner (at noon) or supper (at night) as a sort of dessert with cornbread or "starter" bread, fried apples were always a special addition to my mother's copious farm meals. These are a perfect accompaniment for egg dishes.

—Joe

serves 8-10

1/4	cup butter or margarine
2	tablespoons cinnamon bits (optional)
6-8	cups sliced apples* (do not peel)
1/2	cup brown sugar

Place 10-inch skillet over medium heat. Add butter and cinnamon bits. Add apples and cover with sugar. Cover with lid and cook until apples have released their juice and sugar has dissolved. Partially remove lid and continue cooking until juice has almost disappeared. Cook a total of approximately 20 minutes. I generally don't stir the apples, but if you feel you must, do so gently so the slices will stay intact better.

*Use Jonathan or similar apple. Red is important for color and a firm apple is necessary to avoid mushing.

Birch Creek Inn

2263 Birch Creek Road, De Pere, WI 54115
414-336-7575

Hostess: Jeanette Flener Kosky

Built in 1918, our renovated barn fascinates guests with its heavy, rough hewn beams and ladders to the 40-foot-high cedar ceiling.

The dining area in the lower level, where cows were once milked, features stone walls with exposed beams and planking from the Green Bay Packers' Lambeau Stadium.

The spacious bedrooms have queen- or king-size beds and private baths, one with a double whirlpool.

Overlooking a scenic pond about 10 miles south of the Green Bay city center and near Hilly Haven Golf Course, Birch Creek Inn combines the peace and beauty of the country with the conveniences of the city.

Rates at the Birch Creek Inn range from $55–$79.
Rates include a full breakfast on weekends and
a continental breakfast on weekdays.

K-Bars

K-Bars are quick and easy to prepare.
Since chocolate is a favorite of mine anytime of the day,
K-Bars can be served for that chocolate fix at breakfast
or with tea in the afternoon or evening.

makes 25 or more bars

8	cups Kellogg's Special K cereal
1^1/$_3$	cups corn syrup
1^1/$_3$	cups sugar
1^1/$_3$	cups peanut butter
2	7-ounce chocolate candy bars (I prefer Hershey)

Butter a 9x13-inch pan; set aside. Pour cereal in large mixing bowl; set aside.

Combine syrup and sugar in saucepan. Over medium-high heat, bring to a boil, stirring occasionally. Remove from heat. Mix in peanut butter. Pour over cereal and mix together. Press mixture in buttered pan.

Melt chocolate candy bars in a small saucepan over medium heat and spread over bars.

Brennan Manor Bed & Breakfast

1079 Everett Road, Eagle River, WI 54521
715-479-7353

Hosts: Robert and Connie Lawton

*T*he next time you'd like to get away for awhile, consider spoiling yourself by staying at Brennan Manor, one of Wisconsin's most unique bed and breakfast inns, located in Eagle River, Wisconsin.

Built in the 1920's during the era of the great lumber barons, Brennan Manor offers a luxurious, relaxing atmosphere with old world charm. A genuine suit of armor will welcome you at the front door of this stately English Tudor, complete with hand-carved woodwork, balconies, and arched windows.

We offer a selection of four lavishly decorated rooms, each with private bath, including the romantic "Juliet" room. All bedrooms lead to an open balcony overlooking the spacious Great Room.

When you visit Brennan Manor, we'll bend over backwards to give you superior service and make your visit a special one.

Rates at the Brennan Manor Bed & Breakfast range from $69-$89.
Rates include a full breakfast.

English Breakfast Scones

This recipe is ridiculously simple.
The scones are superior to any other recipe I have tried.
My guests rave about them.

makes 12 scones

2³/₄   cups flour
6   tablespoons sugar
1¹/₂   tablespoons baking powder
1   teaspoon salt
¹/₂   cup chilled butter, diced
1   cup chilled whipping cream or half-and-half
2   large eggs
        Additional sugar for tops of scones

Preheat oven to 400 degrees. Lightly flour baking sheet.

Sift flour, sugar, baking powder, and salt into large bowl. Using pastry cutter, cut butter into flour mixture until it resembles coarse meal.

Whisk cream and eggs in small bowl to blend. Pour over crumb mixture, stirring just until combined. Transfer dough to lightly floured work surface. Form dough into 1-inch thick circle. Cut out scones using a 3-inch round cookie cutter. Transfer scones to prepared baking sheet and sprinkle with sugar.

Bake 10 minutes at 400 degrees. Reduce temperature to 350 degrees and continue baking until light brown, approximately 15-18 minutes. Cool slightly before serving.

The Inn at Pinewood

1800 Silver Forest Lane, P.O. Box 549, Eagle River, WI 54521
715-479-4114

Hosts: Edward and Nona Soroosh

Warmest hospitality awaits you the minute you arrive at The Inn at Pinewood. This delightful 20-room inn has all the charm the north woods has to offer.

The log lodge was purchased by the Sorooshes in 1969 for a boy's camp; then in 1974 they founded Pinewood Academy, a boarding school for dyslexic boys.

Today the Inn retains all the charm of its past. Eight romantic guest rooms all have private baths, king-size beds, balconies overlooking the lake or woods, and some have double whirlpool baths and fireplaces. Guests wake up to the aroma of freshly-baked muffins and breads and enjoy a scrumptious full breakfast.

*Rates at The Inn at Pinewood range from $75-$110.
Rates include a full breakfast.*

Baked Apple Pancake

*Baked Apple Pancake is one of my guests' favorite
breakfasts. Nothing could be simpler than putting all of the
ingredients except the apples and butter in a blender.
The combination of crisp apples and custard, sprinkled with
brown sugar, not only tastes scrumptious but will bring
oh's and ah's from your guests as you bring this
puffy creation from the oven to the table.*

serves 10

6 large eggs	1/4 teaspoon cinnamon (more if
1 1/2 cups milk	desired up to 1 teaspoon)
1 cup flour	1/2 cup butter or margarine
3 tablespoons granulated sugar	2 large Granny Smith apples
1 teaspoon vanilla extract	3 tablespoons brown sugar
1/2 teaspoon salt	

Place eggs, milk, flour, granulated sugar, vanilla, salt, and cinnamon
in blender. Set aside. Put butter or margarine in a 9x 13-inch glass baking dish. Place in 425-degree oven to melt. (Don't let it burn.) Remove
from oven when melted.

Peel apples, slice thinly, and arrange in bottom of dish over melted
butter. Put in oven until butter sizzles. Remove. Blend ingredients in
blender until smooth. Pour slowly over apples. Sprinkle with brown
sugar.

Bake in 425-degree oven for 20 minutes. Test for doneness by
inserting a knife in center. If it comes out clean, it is done. Cut in serving portions and serve immediately. Pass the maple syrup if desired.

The Olde Parsonage
Bed & Breakfast

120 Swift Street, P.O. Box 269, Edgerton, WI 53534
608-884-6490

Hostess: Connie Frank

Retreat to this well-preserved parsonage, built in 1906 for the priests of St. Joseph Church. This historic home is graced with the original oak woodwork, herring bone floors, leaded glass windows, and a porcelain bubbler.

Relax in the parlor with cozy conversation or play euchre in the reading room. Retire to one of four rooms named for my ancestors. Each room is adorned with antiques and family heirlooms. After a restful repose, arise to partake of a hearty continental breakfast.

The Olde Parsonage is located 2 miles off I-90 in the rolling hills of southern Wisconsin in the heart of Edgerton.

Rates at The Olde Parsonage Bed & Breakfast range from $45–$75.
Rates include a continental breakfast.

Zucchini Bread

A delicious, hearty bread served at breakfast, snack time, or with dinner. Try it spread with cream cheese anytime. Now I await the zucchini harvest in late summer to grate and freeze it for baking later.

makes 2 loaves

3	eggs	1/4	teaspoon baking powder
1	cup oil	1	teaspoon baking soda
2	cups sugar	1	tablespoon cinnamon
1	tablespoon vanilla extract	2	cups peeled, grated zucchini
3	cups flour	1/2	cup chopped pecans
1	teaspoon salt		

In large bowl, beat eggs, oil, sugar, and vanilla together.

In separate bowl, sift flour with salt, baking powder, baking soda, and cinnamon. Add flour mixture to egg mixture and beat well. Fold in zucchini and nuts. Divide batter between 2 greased 9x5x3-inch loaf pans.

Bake at 325 degrees for 1 hour. Remove from pan and cool on wire rack. Slice and serve now or wrap and freeze for another day.

Ye Olde Manor House
Bed & Breakfast

N7622 State Road 12, Elkhorn, WI 53121
414-742-2450

Hosts: Babette and Marvin Henschel

Our early twentieth century Manor House, on three woodsy acres across the road from Lauderdale Lakes, is the perfect "home away from home" to relax.

All summer and winter sports are available nearby, with the Kettle Moraine State Forest only four miles from our door.

We generally join our guests for breakfast and hear "rave reviews" on our culinary efforts. With lots of freshly ground coffee and stimulating conversation, strangers become friends at our breakfast table.

Rates at Ye Olde Manor House Bed & Breakfast range from $50–$90. Rates include a full breakfast.

"Never Fail" Cheese Souffle

*This make-ahead souffle recipe was given to us
by my husband's former secretary, Lorma Richmond.
Our guests praise it beyond words.
It is one of our "easy" breakfast treats.*

serves 8

10	slices Pepperidge Farm-type white bread
1/2	cup butter or margarine
10	ounces Old English Cheese (I use Kraft)
2 1/2	cups milk
1	rounded teaspoon dry mustard
	Salt, optional
5	eggs, beaten

Spray 8-inch souffle dish, with 3-inch sides, with non-stick cook-ing spray.

Remove crusts from bread and discard or save for another use. Butter each slice of bread and cut into 1-inch squares. Cut cheese into 1-inch squares. Alternate bread and cheese in souffle dish and fill almost to top.

Mix together milk, mustard, salt, and beaten eggs; pour over bread and cheese. Cover with plastic wrap and place in refrigerator overnight. Remove from refrigerator 1 hour before placing in pre-heated 350-degree oven. Bake 1 hour. Let stand 5 minutes before serving.

Serve with thick, sliced crisp bacon or Canadian bacon and currant scones.

Neenah Creek Inn & Pottery

W7956 Neenah Road, Endeavor, WI 53930
608-587-2229

Hosts: Pat and Doug Cook

*T*he Neenah Creek Inn & Pottery is a turn-of-the-century "Portage" brick house nestled in beautifully landscaped, rolling hills along the Neenah Creek. Wildlife abound all during the year, with sandhill cranes and geese gathering in the fields every fall. Guests can enjoy skiing at nearby Cascade Mountain in Portage or visit the many attractions in Wisconsin Dells, about 14 miles away.

Outdoor porches and a terrace surrounded by a stone wall, as well as 11 acres with walking paths bordered with trees, shrubs, benches, flowers, and herbs along the Neenah Creek, beckon you to explore.

Pat and Doug Cook are your hosts. Doug is a potter and woodcarver, and his stoneware pottery is available for sale. Neenah Creek Inn is a no smoking, no alcohol, no pets facility. Pat is a gourmet cook serving an evening snack and a full breakfast.

Rates at the Neenah Creek Inn & Pottery range from $65–$105.
Rates include a full breakfast.

Grilled Chicken Kabobs

*This is a low calorie, nutritious entree that is attractive
and delicious at any meal. It may be served with rice for
lunch or dinner. At Neenah Creek Inn, we often serve it for
breakfast with toasted homemade bread served with straw-
berry/rhubarb jam, a plate of assorted cheeses, caramel-
pecan rolls, butter, and orange juice.*

serves 6

1	pound deboned chicken breast
1/2	cup fat-free Italian salad dressing
1/2	red bell pepper
1/2	green bell pepper
8	ounces fresh mushrooms
1	20-ounce can of pineapple chunks, drained
	Bamboo skewers or metal kabob skewers

The day before serving, cut chicken into 2x1-inch chunks. Place in a plastic container and sprinkle with Italian dressing. Cover and refrigerate for several hours, stirring occasionally or turning upside down several times.

Cut red and green peppers into 2x1-inch strips. Place in small saucepan over medium heat with water and cook, covered, until tender but still firm. Clean mushrooms.

Thread chunks on skewers as follows: chicken, pineapple, green pepper, pineapple, mushroom, pineapple, red pepper, pineapple, and chicken. Kabobs can be assembled the night before and stored in covered container in refrigerator.

Cook on grill or broil in oven until chicken is browned and cooked.

The French Country Inn of Ephraim

3052 Spruce Lane, P.O. Box 129, Ephraim, WI 54211
414-854-4001

Hosts: Walt Fisher and Joan Fitzpatrick

*I*f you want to experience what vacationing in Door County was like in the 1920's, come stay a few days with us. All our guest rooms have wonderful windows that open to catch the bay breezes and the perfumes of the flower gardens. Large gathering rooms and a magnificent stone fireplace add to the friendly atmosphere. A healthful breakfast concentrating on fruits and grains is served each morning.

Rates at The French Country Inn of Ephraim range from $55–$87.
Rates include a continental breakfast;
egg and meat dishes are not served.

Dates & Millet

This is a wonderful alternate breakfast cereal which is naturally sweet. It has much the same texture as rice pudding when served with milk. It's very nutritional too.

serves 8-12

1   cup millet
1   cup date pieces
3   cups boiling water

"Toast" millet in a dry skillet on the stove top over medium heat. Millet will turn from yellow to light brown or toast colored. Stir occasionally for even browning.

Combine millet, date pieces, and water in a 1-quart baking dish. Bake, covered, in 350-degree oven for 40 minutes. Remove from oven and let stand covered at least 30 minutes before serving.

"Fluff" with a fork while transferring mixture from baking dish to serving bowl. Prepare ahead and refrigerate or serve warm or at room temperature. Serve with milk or milk substitute such as soy milk.

The Birchwood Bed & Breakfast

9121 Spring Road, Fish Creek, WI 54212
414-868-3214

Hosts: Bob and Mary Henke

You are invited to enjoy a peaceful stay in our beautiful home located in Door County, the recreation capital of the Midwest. Our contemporary home is located in a quiet wooded setting a few minutes from the town of Fish Creek and five minutes from many of the recreations available in Door County. There is hiking in the state park or over scenic country roads, some of the finest dining to be found anywhere, and shopping to please the most discriminating and fun-loving. Boating, swimming, biking, music, and entertainment abound, and challenging golf courses are only minutes away. Beauty and breathtaking scenery are readily found to enrich the spirit and inspire the artist. We will be happy to help you plan an exciting, action-filled day, or find a quiet spot to catch up on your reading. At day's end, a peaceful rest is yours in nature's most beautiful surroundings.

Rates at The Birchwood Bed & Breakfast range from $70–$85.
Rates include a full breakfast.

Irish Soda Bread

*This was my grandmother's recipe lovingly made
by my mother and now my own daughter too.
It is wonderful for breakfast or afternoon tea,
and can be kept frozen and used as needed.*

makes 1 loaf

2	cups flour
2	tablespoons sugar
1 1/2	teaspoons baking powder
1/2	teaspoon baking soda
3	tablespoons butter or margarine
1	cup buttermilk
1/2	cup seedless raisins
1/2	teaspoon caraway seeds, optional

Preheat oven to 350 degrees.

In a large bowl, mix flour, sugar, baking powder, and baking soda. Cut in butter or margarine until mixture resembles coarse crumbs. Stir in buttermilk; mix until all ingredients are moistened. Add raisins and caraway seeds.

Gently knead dough on lightly floured board for several minutes, then shape into round loaf. Place loaf in greased 8-inch cake pan.

Bake 40-50 minutes until loaf sounds hollow when tapped on top. Turn out and cool on wire rack.

The Whistling Swan Inn

4192 Main Street, P.O. Box 193, Fish Creek, WI 54212
414-868-3442

Hosts: Jan and Andy Coulson

Located in the heart of Fish Creek, The Whistling Swan Inn is Door County's oldest operating inn. Built in Marinette, Wisconsin, in 1887, it was moved across the ice of Green Bay in 1907 to its current site. Totally renovated by current owners Jan and Andy Coulson in 1985, the inn has seven meticulously decorated rooms and suites, each with coordinating wallpapers and fabrics, all with private bathrooms. Antique carved beds and dressers add to the elegant, yet comfortable decor. The spacious and high-ceilinged lobby has a white mantled fireplace, arched bay windows, and the original restored baby grand piano.

A full breakfast is included and served in the summer on the wide veranda, with its original wicker furniture and splendid view of Fish Creek. During the winter months, a full breakfast is served at The White Gull Inn, one block away.

Rates at The Whistling Swan Inn range from $95–$127. Rates include a full breakfast.

Door County Cherry Sour Cream Coffee Cake

Here in Door County we have a propensity for cherries as they're harvested from our orchards each July. This recipe, however, tastes great with any number of different fruits or a combination of several. Another favorite of our guests is blueberry.

serves 12

2	cups sour cream	2	teaspoons vanilla extract
2	teaspoons baking soda	2	cups frozen cherries, thawed
4	cups flour		and drained
1	tablespoon baking powder	Topping:	
1	cup butter, softened	1¹/₂	cups brown sugar
1¹/₂	cups sugar	2	tablespoons cinnamon
4	eggs	3/4	cup chopped walnuts

Preheat oven to 350 degrees.

To make topping, combine brown sugar, cinnamon, and walnuts. Set aside.

In small bowl, combine sour cream and baking soda. In separate bowl, combine flour and baking powder. In medium mixing bowl, cream butter and sugar together. Add eggs and vanilla; cream until fluffy. Add sour cream and flour mixtures alternately and mix thoroughly.

Spread one half of mixture in greased 9x13-inch pan. Sprinkle cherries over this base layer, then sprinkle 1/3 of topping over the cherries. Spread the other half of the batter on top and sprinkle with remaining topping.

Bake 60-75 minutes. Cover with foil after 30 minutes if top is browning too quickly.

The White Gull Inn

4225 Main Street, P.O. Box 160, Fish Creek, WI 54212
414-868-3517

Hosts: Andy and Jan Coulson

Andy and Jan Coulson, innkeepers at this authentic 1896 hostelry since 1972, have done everything possible to preserve and add to the historic charm of the White Gull. Antiques abound in the common areas as well as the guest rooms, which include many of the original beds and dressers of the first innkeeper, Dr. Herman Welcker. Bedrooms and cottages, most of which have their own fireplace, are decorated in period wallpapers and fabrics characteristic of the turn-of-the-century, with hardwood and pine floors and little touches that make a guest's stay as comfortable as can be.

The inn's dining room, open to the public, is justifiably famous for its traditional Door County fish boils, hearty breakfasts and lunches, and quiet, candlelight dinners. The White Gull has been voted a favorite destination of the readers of *Wisconsin Trails* and *Midwest Living* magazines and has been included on the *Milwaukee Journal's* list of the 25 best Wisconsin restaurants.

Rates at The White Gull Inn range from $85–$160.
A full breakfast is available in the dining room and
is not included in the rates.

Cherry Stuffed French Toast

Cherry Stuffed French Toast has fast become a White Gull Inn favorite. As impressive as it looks (and tastes!), it's an easy one to make at home.

serves 4

1   loaf unsliced egg bread
1   8-ounce package cream cheese, at room temperature
1/3 cup heavy cream
1   cup red tart Door County cherries, drained
6   eggs, well beaten
     Cinnamon
     Powdered sugar, garnish

Slice egg bread into 1½-inch slices. Cut each slice down 3/4 of its length so that you have almost formed two slices of bread, but the bottom 1/4 still holds the entire piece together. Set aside.

Beat cream cheese, heavy cream, and cherries together on medium speed until well combined.

Spread approximately 1/4 cup of the mixture into the pocket of each slice and press the slice together very gently, distributing the filling evenly.

Dip each slice of stuffed egg bread lightly into beaten eggs to coat all sides. Place immediately onto a lightly oiled griddle.

Sprinkle lightly with cinnamon and turn when golden brown. After frying the second side until golden, remove each slice to a cutting board, and very gently slice each piece in half diagonally. To garnish, sprinkle with powdered sugar. Arrange the triangles on plates and serve immediately with maple syrup.

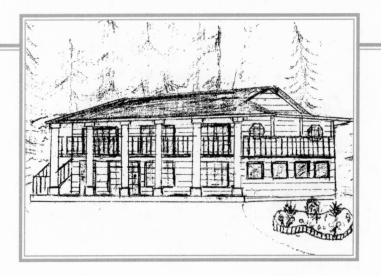

Lakeside Bed & Breakfast

509 Furnace Street, Fisher Lake, P.O. Box 54, Florence, WI 54121
715-528-3259

Hosts: Ron and Rita McMullen

At Lakeside, you'll find homemade Amish quilts and furniture, great lake views from decks and the screened porch, hot tub and exercise room for unwinding, and a delicious hot five-course breakfast served by candlelight. All bedrooms have a private bath and six have fireplaces.

There are many activities in the area: canoeing, paddle boating, fishing, and tubing on the lake and rivers. Snowmobile and cross-country ski trails are right on Fisher Lake. Or just lie back and enjoy the peace and tranquility of a small town.

Rates at the Lakeside Bed & Breakfast range from $70–$100.
Rates include a full breakfast.

Fruit Delight

This really starts the breakfast off with a romantic touch.
Don't forget to light the candles.

serves 6-7

1	small bunch purple grapes
2	red apples, cubed
1	green apple, cubed
1	large banana, sliced
3/4	cup light sour cream or yogurt
1	teaspoon vanilla extract
4	tablespoons maple syrup

Combine grapes, apples, and bananas in medium bowl. In small bowl, combine sour cream, vanilla, and maple syrup and stir to blend.

Pour sour cream mixture over fruit and fold to coat. Refrigerate for at least 1 hour. Serve in a pretty compote dish.

Lamp Post Inn

408 South Main Street, Fort Atkinson, WI 53538
414-563-6561

Hosts: Debbie and Mike Rusch

For a home-away-from-home, come to our warm, cozy Inn. We provide a night of relaxation surrounded by things of the past. Stroll through the flower gardens that surround our home in the summer, or warm yourself by the crackling fireplace in the dead of winter. Each room contains its own antique phonograph for your listening pleasure, and in one of our bathrooms, guests enjoy a jacuzzi for two with skylight.

For adventures near the Lamp Post Inn, we suggest Fireside Dinner Theater Playhouse, Mustang Manor Riding Stables, and Fort Boat Tours.

Rates at the Lamp Post Inn range from $60–$85.
Rates include a full breakfast.

Sorbet

Simple to make—tastes delicious!
A melt-in-your-mouth summer treat.

serves 12

3	pints strawberries (or substitute raspberries)
2	cups sugar
1½	cups orange juice (low acid can be used)
¼	cup reconstituted lemon juice
⅓	cup Grand Marnier, optional

Wash berries, hull, and place in a large bowl. Add sugar, orange juice, lemon juice, and Grand Marnier. Let stand 3 hours at room temperature. Place in blender and blend until smooth. Pour into approximately 3 ice cube trays and freeze.

Serve cubes frozen or blend cubes until slushy. Keep frozen until ready to use.

McConnell Inn

497 South Lawson Drive, P.O. Box 639, Green Lake, WI 54941
414-294-6430

Hosts: Mary Jo and Scott Johnson

Green Lake has a long history of hospitality, being the oldest resort west of Niagara Falls. We are pleased to carry on the tradition in an elegant Victorian, boasting parquet floors, oak woodwork, and leather wainscoting. We offer five guest rooms, each with private bath and queen- or king-size beds. For sumptuous relaxation, our suite features jacuzzi, hearthstone fireplace, 14-foot vaulted ceilings, and sitting room. We serve a hearty, full breakfast prepared by Mary Jo, a pastry chef.

Enjoy Wisconsin's deepest lake, with swimming, boating, and fishing, or partake in golfing, hiking, biking, antiquing, and cross-country skiing.

Rates at the McConnell Inn range from $80–$130.
Rates include a full breakfast.

Apple Cheese Pancakes

*I like to serve these with homemade blueberry and
red cherry syrups. Most guests cannot decipher the
ingredients and are surprised when they hear this recipe.
To make low-fat pancakes, use low-fat cottage cheese and
substitute 7 egg whites for 4 eggs.*

serves 4

1	cup grated fresh apple
1	teaspoon lemon juice
1	tablespoon honey
4	eggs, separated
1	cup cottage cheese
1	cup flour
1	teaspoon cinnamon
1/2	teaspoon salt

In large bowl, mix apple, lemon juice, honey, egg yolks, cottage
cheese, flour, cinnamon, and salt together. Beat egg whites until stiff.
Fold egg whites into batter.

Pour pancakes approximately 3 inches in size on greased, hot griddle
and fry until brown on both sides. Serve with maple syrup and butter.

Summit Farm Bed & Breakfast

1622-110th Avenue, Hammond, WI 54015
715-796-2617

Hosts: Grant and Laura Fritsche

Our bed and breakfast is a comfortable hobby farm tucked in the rolling hills of the St. Croix River Valley. The 1910 farm house has been lovingly restored with today's added comforts. Our guest rooms boast family heirlooms, and the claw-foot bath tubs are deep enough for a good soak.

A full country breakfast is served every morning with many items fresh from our garden and orchard.

The coffee pot is always on; come enjoy our country hospitality.

Rates at the Summit Farm Bed & Breakfast range from $45–$60.
Rates include a full breakfast.

Crab Apple Liqueur

*This spicy liqueur is made each fall from crab apples
from our orchard. It is a Thanksgiving tradition to serve
this after the meal. Visitors may even find it at bed time
on their bedside table.*

makes approximately 1 quart

1   pound red crab apples, approximately
1   cup sugar
2   cups light rum

Wash and remove stems from ripe red crab apples. Cut into quarters. Pack into 1-quart jar up to about 1 inch from top. Add sugar to jar. Pour rum over apples and sugar until jar is full. Place cover on jar and store in a cool, dark place for 30 days. Turn jar every day to combine ingredients.

After 30 days, strain through jelly bag until liquid is clear and pink/red in color. Store in a clean jar. Enjoy!

Edgewater Inn Bed & Breakfast

Turners Road, Route 1 Box 1293, Hayward, WI 54843
715-462-9412

Hosts: Ron and Wendy Rudd

Our 1905 farmhouse is on the shores of the Spider Lake Chain and offers guests a year-round picturesque view, access to endless activities, and quiet solitude. Edgewater Inn is located only five kilometers from the world famous Birkie and CAMBA trails, and the area offers both cross-country and downhill skiing, biking, hiking, golf, canoeing, fishing, swimming, horseback riding, and snowmobiling. Various wildlife visit daily.

Guests enjoy a full taste-bud-popping breakfast and five guest rooms, all with private baths. If rest, relaxation, or recreation is your pleasure, the Edgewater Inn is the perfect destination.

Rates at the Edgewater Inn Bed & Breakfast range from $65–$90. Rates include a full breakfast.

Oatmeal Pudding

*An energizing dish to warm you
on those cool northwoods mornings.*

serves 4

2	cups milk
3	tablespoons brown sugar, divided
1	tablespoon butter
1/4	teaspoon salt
1/4	teaspoon cinnamon
1	cup rolled oats
1/2	cup peeled, diced pear
1/2	cup peeled, diced apple
1/2	cup raisins

Combine milk, 2 tablespoons brown sugar, butter, salt, and cinnamon in a pan. Scald. Add oats, pear, apple, and raisins; heat until bubbles appear at edge of pan. Turn into greased 1 1/2-quart baking dish. Bake at 350 degrees for 30 minutes. After first 15 minutes, stir and add remaining brown sugar.

Lumberman's Mansion Inn

205 East 4th Street, P.O. Box 885, Hayward, WI 54843
715-634-3012

Hosts: Jan Hinrichs Blaedel and Wendy Hinrichs Sanders

Our elegantly restored 1887 Queen Anne Victorian is furnished with antiques but offers modern comforts of whirlpool tubs, queen-size beds, private baths with all rooms, televisions, VCRs, and telephones. Our gourmet breakfasts feature regional delicacies, all prepared from scratch in our kitchen.

The welcome aroma of fresh-baked goods will greet you when you arrive and when you awaken in the morning…just as they did from our mother's kitchen while we were growing up in the Hayward area!

Please join us; you'll find our service, cleanliness, quality, friendliness, privacy, and relaxation are guaranteed in the woods and water paradise of the Hayward Lakes area! Cross-country and downhill skiing, bicycling, hiking, and snowmobiling are nearby on beautiful, well-groomed, woodland trails; canoeing, boating, shopping, crafts, and antiques are all close to our door.

Rates at the Lumberman's Mansion Inn range from $75–$100.
Rates include a full breakfast.

Crispy Cookie Coffee Cakes

Crispy Cookie Coffee Cakes is a reliable, easy-to-make refrigerator dough. They were first made by Jan when she, as a teenager, made delectable baked goods to sell to the guests at our grandparent's resort on Grindstone Lake in Hayward. She would take orders the day before and rise early (a good bed & breakfast habit to develop!) to mix, knead, raise, and bake these homemade delights. The resort guests loved to savor them with their breakfast, as will you!

makes 2-3 dozen rolls

1	package dry yeast	1	cup margarine
1/4	cup plus 2 teaspoons sugar, divided	2	eggs, beaten
1/4	cup warm water (105-115 degrees)	1	cup milk, scalded, cooled to lukewarm
4	cups flour, sifted		Filling:
1	teaspoon grated lemon rind	1	cup sugar
1	teaspoon salt	1	tablespoon cinnamon

In small bowl, combine yeast, 2 teaspoons sugar, and water; set aside.

In large bowl, combine flour, lemon rind, 1/4 cup sugar, and salt. Cut in margarine with a fork. Set aside.

Add beaten eggs and cooled milk to yeast mixture. Add to flour in the large bowl. Stir just to combine; cover tightly. Refrigerate overnight or up to 3 days.

When needed, divide dough in half. Roll out each half on a floured board into a 12x18-inch rectangle. Combine cinnamon and sugar for filling. Sprinkle dough with filling. Roll up and cut into 1-inch slices. Place cut side down on greased cookie sheet and flatten slightly with the palm of your hand. Bake at 400 degrees for 12-15 minutes. When cool, cakes may be frosted with a powdered sugar and milk frosting.

Mustard Seed Bed & Breakfast/ Chez Gervais

262 California Avenue, Hayward, WI 54843
715-634-2908

Hosts: Marty and Mary Gervais

As cross-country ski coaches from Colorado, we wanted to be close to great skiing! Our 18-month search ended in the purchase of the Mustard Seed. We are pleased to be back in the North with its greenness, hardwood forests, and lakes.

We offer shuttle and guide services (and Inn to Inn packages) for skiers, bikers, and hikers. We provide an ambiance geared to relaxation after outdoor activity: pampering in our indoor and outdoor massaging spas, romantic picnics at a nearby pond and park, and lovely walks to downtown shopping and dining. Our cooking reflects our French background and Southwestern travels. We have five totally unique rooms, one suite, two fireplaces, a fenced garden yard, and three spas. "You're only a stranger once."

Rates at the Mustard Seed Bed & Breakfast range from $55–$85.
Rates include a full breakfast.

Breakfast Burritos

This recipe originated in our restaurant in Colorado.
It can be made ahead and frozen before baking.
Egg Beaters and yogurt can be substituted for low
cholesterol diets, and a vegetarian option is easy by
substituting black beans for Chorizo!
Even those who "don't like spicy food" love it!

serves 6

2	pounds browned Chorizo sausage	1/2	teaspoon cilantro	
12	eggs	6	medium soft shell tortillas	
1/2	cup onions		(either flour or corn)	
1	tomatilla	3	cups grated cheddar cheese	
1	4-ounce can chopped green chilies	1	cup sour cream	
1	4-ounce can olives	2	cups salsa	
1/2	teaspoon garlic powder	2	cups guacamole	

Brown Chorizo in bite-size pieces (you may substitute Italian or other sausage if you can't find Chorizo). Whip together eggs with one eggshell of water. Scramble eggs. Saute onions and chopped tomatilla; mix in chilies, olives, garlic, and cilantro. Stir vegetable mixture and sausage into scrambled eggs.

Fill each tortilla with egg/meat mixture, roll shell to form burrito, and place seam side down in 9x12-inch baking pan. Top each with 1/2 cup cheese. Bake at 375 degrees for 15 minutes. Serve with sour cream, salsa, and guacamole.

Jefferson-Day House

1109-3rd Street, Hudson, WI 54016
715-386-7111

Hosts: Sharon and Wally Miller

uilt in 1857 on a quiet, tree-lined street two blocks from the St. Croix River, the Jefferson-Day House is a comfortable combination of old and new. The inn is furnished with antiques, Maxfield Parrish prints, lace curtains, and handmade quilts. Each individually decorated room has a queen-size bed, air conditioning, private bath, and double whirlpool tub; three of the four rooms have gas fireplaces.

Breakfast at the Jefferson-Day is a total experience, from the large bowl of fresh fruit and home-baked muffins to the main entree and dessert. Wally often serenades guests by playing his guitar and singing the dessert song.

Rates at the Jefferson-Day House range from $99–$169;
single's rates available.
Rates include a full breakfast.

Oven Omelette

*"Creativity" is the key to this quick and easy recipe.
Make it your own by substituting or adding other vegetables
and meats, using Egg Beaters, or trying a variety of cheeses
such as cheddar, Swiss, or Gouda. Saute vegetables in cooking spray rather than grease to reduce fat.*

serves 6

8	slices bacon, crumbled	6	eggs
1/4	cup green onion, chopped	1	cup milk
3/4	cup tomatoes, seeds removed and diced	1¼	cups shredded cheese, divided
1	tablespoon flour	1	tablespoon Parmesan cheese, finely grated
1/2	teaspoon salt		

Cook bacon until crispy; drain and crumble. Reserve 1 tablespoon bacon grease and use to saute onions until tender. Add tomatoes; sprinkle with flour and salt and stir until coated.

Beat eggs and milk in large bowl. Add vegetables, 1 cup shredded cheese, and crumbled bacon.

Pour mixture into 9-inch glass dish greased with butter. Sprinkle with Parmesan cheese. Bake at 350 degrees for 25-30 minutes. Remove from oven and immediately sprinkle with remaining 1/4 cup shredded cheese. Let stand for 5 minutes before serving.

Phipps Inn

1005 Third Street, Hudson, WI 54016
715-386-0800

Hosts: John and Cyndi Berglund

This romantic 1884 Queen Anne Victorian Inn is located in historic Hudson, a river town nestled along the scenic St. Croix, yet only 20 minutes from the St. Paul/Minneapolis area. The Inn offers three parlors and a formal dining room on the first floor and six private bath suites, all with double whirlpools and most with fireplaces. A lavish and leisurely four-course breakfast is served in the dining room at 9:00 a.m. or in your suite at your request.

Nearby attractions include the Octagon House, the Phipps Theater, St. Croix River, Willow River State Park, hot-air ballooning, shopping, and fine dining.

Step through our door and back across one hundred years into a more graceful era...

Rates at the Phipps Inn range from $89–$179.
Rates include a full breakfast.

Cranberry Muffins with Hot Buttered Rum Sauce

My mother, Joyce, used to make these muffins for her morning church circle groups. They always looked so pretty, smelled so good, and tasted mouth-watering. Needless to say, they gathered rave reviews! An elegant muffin to serve on one of our cold, snowy winter days.

makes 18 muffins

3	tablespoons butter	Buttered Rum Sauce:	
1	cup sugar	$1/2$	cup butter
$1/2$	cup water	2	cups sugar
$1/2$	cup evaporated milk	1	cup evaporated milk
2	cups flour	2	teaspoons vanilla extract
1	teaspoon baking soda		
2	heaping cups whole raw cranberries		

Cream together butter and sugar. Stir in water, evaporated milk, flour, baking soda, and cranberries. Spray muffin tins with cooking spray and fill 2/3 full with batter.

Bake in 350-degree oven for 20-25 minutes.

To make sauce, combine ingredients and heat to almost boiling in a medium saucepan; pour over muffins to serve.

Iris Inn

385 North Main Street, P.O. Box 264, Iola, WI 54945
715-445-4848

Hosts: Murnell and Gerald Olsen

The Iris Inn is a 100-year-old landmark in the heart of Iola, a small town in central Wisconsin. The restored, air-conditioned home has four guest bedrooms, two with private baths. It is furnished with antiques and modern furniture blended for comfort. Homemade quilts cover the beds as well as decorate the Inn. The home and the Iola area lend itself to stress relief and relaxation with four seasons of quiet, beautiful surroundings and is an excellent area for the "silent sports" enthusiasts. Golf, theaters, shopping, and excellent restaurants are within a few minutes' drive. In the true tradition of bed and breakfast, you will enjoy warm hospitality, a relaxed atmosphere, a pot of hot coffee outside your room in the morning, and a full breakfast served in the dining room.

Rates at the Iris Inn range from $35-$65.
Rates include a full breakfast.

Orange Cranberry Muffins

*This recipe can be partially prepared the night before and is
especially complementary with a serving of fresh fruit.
For a variation of this recipe, substitute 1 tablespoon
poppy seeds for cranberries.*

makes 12 medium or 18-20 mini-muffins

2	cups flour	1	cup buttermilk
1/2	cup sugar	6	tablespoons butter or margarine,
1	teaspoon baking powder		room temperature
1	teaspoon baking soda	2	eggs
1/4	teaspoon salt	1/2	cup cranberries, cut in half
1/2	medium orange, peeled,	1/4	cup chopped nuts, optional
	chopped, seeds removed		

In large bowl, whisk to combine flour, sugar, baking powder, baking
soda, and salt. Place orange, buttermilk, butter, and eggs in blender.
Blend at low speed until orange appears to be grated. Pour orange mixture into dry mixture. Mix just until all ingredients are moistened. Fold
in cranberries and nuts.

Grease muffin pan or use paper cups. Fill muffin cups 3/4 full. Bake
in 375-degree oven for 20 minutes for medium muffins, 12-14 minutes
for mini-muffins.

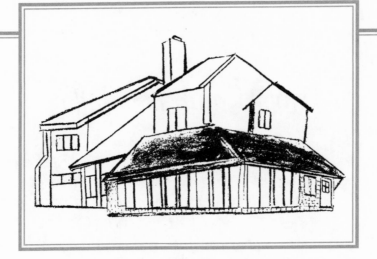

Country Retreat on Primrose Lane

N4589 Primrose Lane, Juneau, WI 53039
414-386-2912

Hostess: Sally Momberg

*L*eave your fast pace behind when you enter this sprawling contemporary home nestled in the Dodge County glacial drumlins. Whether you prefer a romantic getaway or a group outing, you are certain to find yourself immersed in relaxation. For your enjoyment we offer gardens, prairie, outside pool and hot tub, bicycles, pool table, exercise equipment, sauna, fireplace, sun room with wet bar and much, much more.

We're located just minutes from Wild Goose State Trail, Horicon Marsh, and golf courses.

Rates at the Country Retreat on Primrose Lane range from $36–$95.
Rates include a full breakfast.

Streusel Coffee Cake

*I like to bake this in the early evening
as it fills the house with smells of what's to come.*

serves 10-12

2	cups cake flour		Streusel Topping:
1	cup sugar	1½	cups graham cracker crumbs
2½	teaspoons baking powder	¾	cup finely chopped walnuts
½	teaspoon salt	¾	cup brown sugar, firmly
½	cup butter, room temperature		packed
2	eggs	1	teaspoon ground cinnamon
1½	teaspoons vanilla extract	¼	teaspoon ground cardamom
1	cup milk	½	cup butter, melted

Butter and flour 10-inch tube pan.

Make streusel topping by combining graham cracker crumbs, walnuts, brown sugar, cinnamon, cardamom, and butter in medium bowl. Blend well; set aside.

Sift cake flour, sugar, baking powder, and salt in large bowl. Add butter, eggs, vanilla, and milk. Beat vigorously by hand until smooth, about 1 minute. Spread half the batter in buttered pan. Sprinkle half streusel mix over batter. Spoon remaining batter over streusel, then top with remaining streusel.

Bake at 350 degrees about 50 minutes. Insert wooden toothpick into center—it will come out clean when done. Cool 20 minutes, then remove from pan.

Trillium

Route 2 Box 121, LaFarge, WI 54639
608-625-4492

Hostess: Rosanne Boyett

This is a private cottage on our family farm. We raise a variety of field crops and keep several types of livestock, plus numerous people-friendly cats and kittens. The cottage is open all year and is fully furnished, complete with its own bath and kitchen. There is a stone fireplace (with wood provided for guests' use) in the living room and a furnace for colder weather. The cottage has a porch across the east end (with porch swing from a neighboring Amish furniture maker) that faces out over woods and fields. It is convenient to our house and the farm buildings but is private and separate, with its own yard of trees, flower beds, picnic table, and grill. There is a hammock in the shade of large trees in the yard.

Rates are by the number of guests per day, with young children staying for no charge. A crib and high chair are provided in the cottage.

Rates at Trillium range from $50–$70.
Rates include a full breakfast.

Scottish Raspberry Buns

*This recipe is a family favorite and reflects my
Scottish heritage from my maternal grandparents.
They came to this country in 1838 from Scotland.
I am fond of this recipe because it can be altered to use
low-fat milk and is made with more than one grain
(both wheat and rice flours are used).*

makes 8 buns

1	cup flour
3/4	cup rice flour
1/2	teaspoon baking powder
	Pinch salt
1/4	cup sugar
4	tablespoons butter
1/4	cup whole milk, tepid
1	large egg
8-10	teaspoons raspberry jam

In medium bowl, sift together flours, baking powder, salt, and sugar. Cut butter into dry ingredients to form crumbly mixture.

In small bowl, stir together milk and egg. Add liquid mixture to dry ingredients and blend.

Form 8 uniform-size balls with dough. Place individual balls on ungreased baking sheet. Indent each ball and fill with approximately 1 teaspoon raspberry jam. Bake in preheated 400-degree oven for 12-15 minutes until lightly browned.

The Swallow's Nest Bed & Breakfast

141 Sarrington, P.O. Box 418, Lake Delton, WI 53940
608-254-6900

Hosts: Mary Ann and Rod Stemo

This new home in a secluded setting is situated one mile off I-90 and I-94. Choose from four guest rooms, each with a private bath, and furnished with family collectibles, many of which are from England. The home features monastery windows, two-story atrium with skylights, library with fireplace, and decks with bird's eye view of Lake Delton. A photography studio and gallery are on the premises. Guests can enjoy a game of pool in the lower level recreation room, and TV is also available.

Area attractions include Wisconsin Dells, Devil's Lake and Mirror Lake state parks, Circus World Museum, downhill and cross country skiing, antique shops, and fine restaurants.

Rates at The Swallow's Nest Bed & Breakfast range from $65-$70.
Rates include a full breakfast.

Fluffy Cheese Omelet

Eggs microwave rapidly, and since they are a delicate food, they toughen when overcooked. The yolks, which have a higher fat content, cook faster than the whites. When yolks and whites are mixed together, eggs may be cooked at higher power settings. Omelets, which need time to set, are cooked at medium (5) while scrambled eggs, which are stirred, are microwaved at high (10).

To serve this omelet, add three pork sausages on the plate, with two orange slices, three kiwi slices, and three slices of fresh strawberries. Serve with fresh squeezed orange juice and fresh ground coffee. Add homemade blueberry muffins on the side in a wicker basket.

serves 4

8 eggs, separated	4 tablespoons butter
Pinch salt	2 cups finely shredded cheddar cheese
6 tablespoons water, divided	Chives and parsley, garnish
2/3 cup low cal mayonnaise	

In large mixer bowl, beat egg whites at highest speed of mixer; add pinch of salt and 2 tablespoons water. In smaller bowl, using same beaters, beat yolks, mayonnaise, and 4 tablespoons water. Gently pour yolk mixture over beaten whites; fold together carefully.

Divide butter between two 9-inch microwavable pie plates. Microwave at high (10) 1 minute, swirl butter to coat dish. Carefully pour egg mixture into pie plates. Microwave at medium 5-6 minutes. Sprinkle cheese over omelets. Microwave at medium 1-2 minutes, until cheese is slightly melted. Quickly run spatula or turner around sides and bottom of dish. Fold omelet in half. Gently slide onto serving plate. Sprinkle with chives and parsley, if desired.

Pederson Victorian Bed & Breakfast

1782 Highway 120 North, Lake Geneva, WI 53147
414-248-9110

Hostess: Kristi Cowles

Just three miles north of Lake Geneva, where quiet back country roads are prevalent and inviting, Pederson Victorian stands tall and majestic. This 1880 Queen Anne is "distinctively different," cleverly blending its authentic, old-world charm with '90's earth-care intelligence in order to make your stay a refreshing experience!

Breakfasts are full, vegetarian and "utterly" delicious. The four guest rooms are filled with creative amenities and antiques. Wonderful porches, a cozy sun room and parlor, backyard hammocks, and lush herb gardens are irresistible…not to mention spirited Scandinavian hospitality and the fresh-air fragrance of line-dried linens (even in winter). Indeed!

*Rates at Pederson Victorian Bed & Breakfast range from
$60–$80. Rates include a full, vegetarian breakfast.*

Kristi's Breakfast Corn Bake

*This is a very versatile dish that can accompany any
main course. I usually serve it with pancakes of a variety
of flavors, such as ginger, raspberry, blueberry, or
oat bran-pecan. It's also delicious with pasta dishes
or vegetable entrees for lunch or dinner.*

serves 8

2	cups corn meal
2	teaspoons baking powder
1	teaspoon salt
1	cup plain non-fat yogurt
1	16-ounce can creamed corn
1/2	cup butter, softened (1/4 cup olive oil and 1/4 cup butter may be substituted)
2	cups whole kernel corn, fresh or frozen
11/2-2	cups grated cheese (I use raw-milk cheddar)

In medium bowl, combine corn meal, baking powder, and salt. In large bowl, combine yogurt, cream corn, butter, and whole kernel corn. Add dry ingredients to wet ingredients.

Scoop equal amount of batter into 2 greased 9-inch pie pans. Sprinkle with equal amounts of cheese. Bake uncovered 40-45 minutes at 350 degrees.

The Fargo Mansion Inn

406 Mulberry Street, Lake Mills, WI 53551
414-648-3654

Hosts: Barry Luce and Tom Boycks

No matter what season, The Fargo Mansion Inn will provide you with the perfect setting for a memorable romantic getaway. Listed on the National Register of Historic Places, The Fargo Mansion Inn has elegantly appointed Victorian guest rooms—all with private baths, some with fireplaces and double whirlpools.

After enjoying a full gourmet breakfast, a day's activities may include hiking or cross-country skiing at Aztalan State Park, boating or swimming on beautiful Rock Lake, or biking the Glacial Drumlin Bike Trail. For the less adventurous, historic downtown Lake Mills provides an array of unique gift, pottery, and antique shops. Come experience us: we have been preparing for your visit for over 100 years!

Rates at The Fargo Mansion Inn range from $72-$165.
Rates include a full breakfast.

Cheese Strata

A great "night-before recipe."
A true time-saver when serving large groups of guests.

serves 8

12	slices white bread	2	tablespoons minced onions
3	cups shredded cheddar cheese	6	eggs, lightly beaten
2	16-ounce packages frozen broccoli, cooked	3½	cups milk
2	cups diced ham or fried bacon	½	teaspoon salt
		¼	teaspoon dry mustard

Cut 12 "donuts and holes" from bread with donut cutter. Set aside. Spray 9x13-inch glass baking dish with cooking spray; fit scraps of bread in bottom. Layer cheese over bread; top with cooked, drained broccoli, then ham or bacon. Sprinkle minced onion over top. Arrange donuts and holes over top. In medium mixing bowl, combine beaten eggs, milk, salt, and dry mustard. Pour over top. Cover and chill for 6 hours or overnight.

Bake uncovered in 325-degree oven for 55 minutes.

Victorian Treasure
Bed & Breakfast Inn

115 Prairie Street, Lodi, WI 53555
608-592-5199

Hosts: Todd and Kimberly Seidl

Experience timeless ambiance, thoughtful amenities, and caring innkeepers at a classic Victorian bed and breakfast inn. Timeless ambiance...1897 Queen Anne architecture, wraparound veranda, stained and leaded glass, pocket doors, gas and electric chandeliers, rich carved woods, and much more. Thoughtful amenities... cotton robes, glycerine soaps, down pillows and comforters, suites with whirlpools and fireplaces. Caring innkeepers... educated and experienced in hotel and restaurant management, exceptional cooks, fussy about the details, and genuinely interested in exceeding guests' expectations.

Located in the scenic Lake Wisconsin recreational area, between Madison and Wisconsin Dells. We look forward to meeting you!

*Rates at the Victorian Treasure Bed & Breakfast Inn
range from $65–$159.
Rates include a full breakfast.*

Kimberly's Strawberry Coffee Cake

*Every cook has one of those "whip-it-up-in-a-jiffy"
company cakes. This one was Kimberly's mother's recipe
taken from an old community cookbook. In her home,
this cake was often found on the breakfast table, coffee table
in the afternoon, or dinner table. It looks like you really
fussed, and they'll never believe how easy it was!
Many variations make it extremely versatile: add sliced
plums and nutmeg, sugar and streusel...the list goes on.
Top the warm cake with frozen yogurt, ice cream, or
whipped cream for a terrific dessert.*

serves 8

1	cup flour	2	tablespoons butter, melted
1/2	cup sugar	11/2	cups fresh strawberries, sliced
2	teaspoons baking powder		
1/2	teaspoon salt		Streusel:
1/2	cup milk	1/2	cup flour
1	egg	1/2	cup sugar
1	teaspoon vanilla extract	1/4	cup butter, softened

In large bowl, mix flour, sugar, baking powder, and salt. Add milk, egg, vanilla, and butter. Stir until well blended. Pour into greased and floured 8-inch springform pan. Top with berries. Make streusel by combining flour, sugar, and butter; sprinkle over berries. Bake at 375 degrees for 30 minutes, or until golden brown and toothpick inserted in cake comes out clean. Slice into 8 wedges and serve.

Harrisburg Inn Bed & Breakfast

W3334 Highway 35, P.O. Box 15, Maiden Rock, WI 54750
715-448-4500

Hosts: Bern Paddock and Carol Crisp (Paddock)

Nowhere in the upper Mississippi valley can one find a more panoramic view than from the windows and porches of the Harrisburg Inn. Every season presents new visual delights to fortunate travelers of the Great River Road along Wisconsin's west coast.

Around Lake Pepin, 12 vintage villages offer unique shopping experiences in all manner of arts and crafts, plus unparalleled antiques. You may pick your own blueberries, raspberries, and apples. Perhaps in May find the elusive morel or cut bittersweet in October. Then, return to the Harrisburg to absorb the grandeur of the sunset and anticipate the morning's fragrant aromas. Come inn-joy with us.

Rates at the Harrisburg Inn Bed & Breakfast range from $58-$88.
Rates include a full breakfast.

Sausage Gravy Harrisburg Style

*This is our version of a southern favorite. We like veggies in the
sauce for flavor as well as color. When serving guests who are not
meat-eaters, we omit the sausage and add chopped fresh parsley
and sometimes sliced water chestnuts. Pillsbury Southern Style
Grands are a great biscuit for this dish and a real time-saver.
We admit to sometimes "just baking, not making."*

serves 8 with some "seconds"

1 pound Italian or Cajun seasoned sausage	White Sauce:
1 pound mild pork sausage	$1/2$ cup butter or margarine
1 cup chopped onion	$1/2$ cup flour
1 cup shredded carrot	$1/4$ teaspoon pepper
1 cup chopped broccoli florets	$1/2$ teaspoon salt
1 cup chopped fresh mushrooms or 1 8-ounce can sliced	1 teaspoon original Mrs. Dash Seasoning (no-salt)
Baking powder biscuits	5 cups milk

Crumble sausage into large electric or range-top skillet. Saute over medium heat until thoroughly cooked, about 15 minutes, stirring to break sausage into small pieces. Drain off accumulated fat. Add onion, carrot, broccoli, and mushrooms in layers over sausage. Cover, turn heat to low, and let vegetables steam for 5 minutes. Remove lid; stir. Cover and keep warm.

For sauce, melt butter over low heat in second skillet. Sprinkle flour over butter a tablespoon at a time. Stir and cook until bubbling and lightly browned. Remove from heat, add seasonings, then milk, pouring slowly and stirring constantly to make a smooth paste. Return to heat and bring to a simmer; cook 3-4 minutes until sauce thickens to desired consistency.

Add white sauce to the sausage-vegetable mixture and blend. Keep hot, covered, over low heat until ready to serve over biscuits.

Arbor Manor Bed & Breakfast

1304 Michigan Avenue, Manitowoc, WI 54220
414-684-6095

Hosts: Lou Ann and Jay Spaanem

This 6,000-square-foot mansion was built in the late 1850's, with additions in 1890 and 1929. Arbor Manor is an elegant example of Neo-Classical (Greek) Revival architecture. Marble floors, fireplaces and vanities, parquet flooring, and decorative plaster accents are usual for this style and time.

All three guest chambers have their own private bathrooms and king- or queen-size beds and are air-conditioned and over-sized. One also has a fireplace for your romantic getaway!

Come, relax, enjoy our hospitality and home. Take the car ferry, tour museums and the lake shore, or enjoy a day trip to Door County!

*Rates at the Arbor Manor Bed & Breakfast range from $90–$95.
Rates include a full breakfast.*

Spiced Apples

This easy to make, do-ahead apple recipe is wonderful served warm in the fall or winter along with coffee, juices, and breads. It also goes with almost any entree and can be garnished with orange mist or chopped pecans instead of the whipped cream. Spiced Apples are just part of the full breakfast served at Arbor Manor.

serves 4

3	tablespoons butter or margarine	Topping:
2	tablespoons red hot cinnamon candies or 2 teaspoons cinnamon	1/2 cup whipping cream
		1 tablespoon sugar
1/3	cup blush grape juice, cherry juice or port wine	1/8 teaspoon ground cinnamon
3	large cooking apples, peeled, cored and sliced into rings	

Place butter in 1¹/₂-quart casserole and microwave on high for 30-45 seconds, until melted. Stir in red hots and grape juice. Add apple slices, one at a time, coating each with the mixture. Cook covered on high for 5-7 minutes or until tender crisp. Stir once or twice during this time so that all slices pick up the pink color.

To make topping, beat cream with sugar and cinnamon until peaks form.

Serve apples and sauce in individual dishes or compote serving dish. Top with a dollop of cream. Sprinkle with additional cinnamon if desired.

The Jarvis House Bed & Breakfast

635 North Seventh Street, Manitowoc, WI 54220
414-682-2103

Hosts: Lisa and James Klein

Built in 1898, this stately home became The Jarvis House Bed and Breakfast in September 1993.

Many antiques and family heirlooms fill the house. Guests have a choice of three guest rooms, one with a private bath, the other two sharing a connecting bath. Special amenities include cotton-terry robes, handmade quilts, plush towels, and turn-down service with Beerntsen's chocolates or other delicacies. Guests have exclusive use of the second floor sitting/TV room and are invited to relax in the spacious living room or on the front porch. The large flower garden is enjoyed by guests and neighbors alike. Guests begin their day with fresh, hot coffee and tea brought up to the landing before all join in for a scrumptious, "skip lunch" breakfast in the dining room.

Manitowoc is the home of the Wisconsin Maritime Museum, Natural Ovens Bakery, Beerntsen's Confectionery with its old fashioned sundaes, sodas, and hand-dipped chocolates, and the Wisconsin Port of the Lake Michigan Carferry.

A great place to get away to for rest, relaxation, and friendly hospitality!

Rates at The Jarvis House range from $65–$75.
Rates include a full breakfast.

Morning Glorious Muffins

*Similar to many recipes, this muffin has a much lower fat
and sugar content; yogurt and applesauce have been added
to create a delicious carrot-apple low-fat muffin. Don't let the
number of ingredients stop you; this muffin is well worth the
time and effort and freezes very well. For chocolate lovers
add 1 cup chocolate chips.*

makes 24 muffins

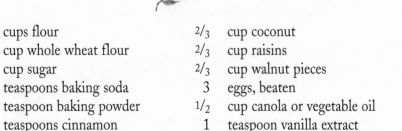

1³/₄	cups flour	2/3	cup coconut
1	cup whole wheat flour	2/3	cup raisins
3/4	cup sugar	2/3	cup walnut pieces
2¹/₂	teaspoons baking soda	3	eggs, beaten
1	teaspoon baking powder	1/2	cup canola or vegetable oil
2¹/₂	teaspoons cinnamon	1	teaspoon vanilla extract
1/2	teaspoon salt	3/4	cup unsweetened applesauce
2 1/3	cups peeled, shredded carrots	3/4	cup plain or vanilla nonfat
2 1/3	cups peeled, shredded apples		yogurt

Preheat oven to 350 degrees. Spray or grease cups of muffin pans.

In medium mixing bowl, combine flours, sugar, baking soda, baking powder, cinnamon, and salt. Set aside.

In large mixing bowl, combine carrots, apples, coconut, raisins, and walnuts. Add eggs, oil, vanilla, applesauce, and yogurt.

Combine flour mixture with ingredients in large mixing bowl. Mix just to moisten dry ingredients.

Divide batter into 24 muffin cups. Bake 20-25 minutes or until tester inserted comes out clean. Remove muffins from pan to wire rack to cool.

Serve with softened or whipped cream cheese.

Hitching Post Bed & Breakfast

N88 W16954 Main Street, Menomonee Falls, WI 53051
414-255-1496

Hostess: Holly M. Smith

The philosophy at the Hitching Post Bed & Breakfast is that everyone deserves special treatment. Upon arrival, complimentary wine, cheese, crackers, and fresh fruit are served in the family room of our 1869 Colonial home. We offer suggestions for nearby dining experiences and describe local attractions, quaint shops, parks, bike trails, and historical museums. Milwaukee is only 20 minutes away.

Guests are greeted in the morning with newspaper, coffee, and juice brought to their room. Breakfast can be served wherever they please...in bed, downstairs in the dining room, or outside on the deck.

Come and indulge. We're waiting to serve you!

Rates at the Hitching Post Bed & Breakfast range from $60-$75.
Rates include a full breakfast.

Syl's Scratzkis

*My late father, Sylvester Wabiszewski, loved to cook and
frequently prepared this hearty breakfast meal
on Sunday mornings for his ten children.
This is one of my guests' favorite dishes.
It is easy to prepare and guaranteed to
put a smile on any face.*

serves 4-6

1	pound bacon, cut into 1-inch strips
1/4	cup diced onions
1	pound fresh mushrooms, sliced
12	eggs, beaten
3/4	cup grated cheese, colby or cheddar

Place sliced bacon into large skillet and fry until browned but not crispy. Turn off heat and drain grease into another container. Leave about 1/4 cup bacon grease in skillet with bacon. Add onions and mushrooms to skillet. Stir constantly until done; onions will appear transparent and white mushrooms brown.

Add beaten eggs and cheese. Stir constantly until eggs are fluffy and done.

Cedar Trail Guesthouse

Route 4 Box 175, Menomonie, WI 54751
715-664-8828

Hosts: Barb Anderson and Diane Duffy

*B*arb and Diane invite you to enjoy the quiet of Dunn County. Barb lives on a nearby farm with her husband, Charlie, and Diane lives at Cedar Trail Guesthouse. Together they operate like a tag team so they can balance home, work, school, and share the fun of meeting and serving their interesting guests.

Cedar Trail Guesthouse is located midway on the Red Cedar State Park Trail, less than 10 minutes from Menomonie and 60 minutes from Minneapolis/St. Paul. The six-level farm house is air-conditioned, has queen-size beds, antiques, and is decorated with hand-pieced comforters filled with wool from Barb's sheep.

Breakfast features local produce, meats, and cheeses. Dunn County produces 85 percent of the kidney beans in the U.S. Finding a way to serve kidney beans was a unique challenge solved by our kidney bean cookie recipe. Guests are encouraged to raid the cookie jar at their leisure.

Rates at the Cedar Trail Guest House range from $45–$65.
Rates include a full breakfast.

Cedar Trail's Kidney Bean Cookies

This is a fun recipe to make because guests have fun guessing what is in it. Dunn County is the top grower of kidney beans so using them in our cookies supports our farmers right here at home. Kidney beans make the cookie soft and help them to keep well in the cookie jar or in the freezer. Canned kidney beans can be used, drained, and pureed.

makes 4 dozen cookies

2	cups dry kidney beans or		1	teaspoon baking soda
	1 15$^{1}/_{2}$-ounce can kidney beans		1	teaspoon baking powder
1	cup brown sugar		1	teaspoon cinnamon
$^{1}/_{3}$	cup shortening		$^{1}/_{2}$	teaspoon cloves
3	eggs		$^{1}/_{2}$	cup chopped nuts, optional
1	cup applesauce		$^{1}/_{2}$	cup raisins, optional
2$^{1}/_{2}$	cups flour		1	cup chocolate chips, optional

Soak kidney beans overnight in water to cover. Rinse and place beans in kettle with enough water to cover beans. Simmer approximately 1 hour until tender; drain. Blend beans in blender to make puree. If using canned beans, place entire contents into blender and blend.

In large bowl, mix bean puree, sugar, shortening, eggs, and applesauce to a creamy texture. Beat until fluffy. Add flour, baking soda, baking powder, cinnamon, and cloves. Beat until smooth. Stir in optional ingredients; you can add just one or all of them.

Drop by teaspoonfuls onto greased cookie sheet. Bake at 350 degrees for 15 minutes or until golden brown. Cool on rack.

The Brick House Bed & Breakfast

108 South Cleveland Street, Merrill, WI 54452
715-536-3230

Hosts: Kris and Randy Ullmer

Sparkling beveled glass doors lead to a glowing fireplace in this prairie-style home. Built in 1915 by the grandfather of actress Tyne ("Cagney and Lacey") Daly, The Brick House Bed & Breakfast is handsomely appointed with a growing collection of Arts and Crafts furnishings.

Merrill's 10 parks beckon walkers and bicyclists to view lush summer greenery or vibrant fall colors. A few steps from the Brick House winds the Wisconsin River. In the white winter, cross-country skiers glide on miles of groomed meandering or challenging trails. A special breakfast begins a day of relaxation or recreation…away from the crowds.

Rates at The Brick House Bed & Breakfast range from $40-$60.
Rates include a full breakfast.

Norwegian Kringler

*Norwegian Kringler takes only 15 minutes to prepare
for baking. For those with dietary restrictions,
this sugar-free pastry is also delicious without the frosting.
At The Brick House, Norwegian Kringler is preceded by
fresh fruits and accompanied by thinly sliced honey ham,
juice, and gourmet coffee.*

serves 4-6

2 cups flour, divided	Frosting:
1 cup butter, divided	$3/4$ cup powdered sugar
1 cup plus 1 tablespoon	1 tablespoon cream
water, divided	1 tablespoon butter, melted
3 eggs	$1/2$ teaspoon almond extract
$1/2$ teaspoon almond extract (or	(or other flavor)
other flavor such as orange)	$1/2$ cup sliced almonds

Stir together 1 cup flour, $1/2$ cup melted butter, and 1 tablespoon water. Lightly press onto bottom and sides of $91/2$- inch round, shallow pan (quiche pan).

Bring to boil $1/2$ cup butter and 1 cup water. Pour into large mixing bowl and stir in 1 cup flour until smooth. Stir in eggs one at a time. Stir in almond extract. Spread batter over crust mixture. Bake at 375 degrees for 1 hour, until medium dark brown.

To make frosting, combine powdered sugar, cream, butter, and extract using electric mixer. Pour into pastry bag (or plastic "baggie" with clipped corner) and frost Kringler using a lattice pattern.

Scatter sliced almonds over frosting. Serve warm.

The Middleton Beach Inn

2303 Middleton Beach Road, Middleton, WI 53562
608-831-6446

Hosts: Brad and Diane Duesler

The early sunshine sparkling on the waters of Lake Mendota is just one of the things that makes breakfast special at The Middleton Beach Inn. Our Broccoli Cheese Strata is just one of the other special treats you can experience.

You're invited to come explore the unique accommodations and enjoy the personal attention and a delicious heartland breakfast along the shores of Madison's largest lake.

Each of the rooms at The Middleton Beach Inn has unique quality and charm. We use soft linens, hand-stitched quilts, oversized towels, and down pillows. Each guest is invited to walk down and enjoy the area's largest athletic facility—The Harbor Athletic Club—as our guest.

Rates at The Middleton Beach Inn range from $65-$145.
Rates include a full breakfast.

Broccoli Cheese Strata

A classic blend of cheese and broccoli baked with a tasty blend of eggs and spices to please the morning palate. Top with salsa to spice up this wonderful treat.

serves 6-8

1/4 cup chopped onion	2 cups shredded cheddar cheese, divided
2 tablespoons butter	
6 large eggs	1 10-ounce package frozen chopped broccoli, uncooked or fresh
2 cups milk	
1 teaspoon Worcestershire sauce	
Salt and pepper to taste	Parsley flakes
12 slices bread (white or wheat)	

Saute onion in butter; remove from heat. Beat eggs with milk. Add sauteed onion, Worcestershire sauce, and salt and pepper to taste.

With a cookie cutter, cut out a shape from the center of bread slices, setting aside shaped bread pieces. Break up remaining pieces of bread and place into a shallow 2-quart glass baking dish. Top with 1 3/4 cups shredded cheese. Layer broccoli evenly over cheese. Place shaped bread pieces on top of broccoli and pour egg/milk mixture over the top. Sprinkle remaining 1/4 cup shredded cheese on top of bread shapes; sprinkle with parsley flakes. Cover and refrigerate at least 2 hours or overnight.

Bake, uncovered in 350-degree oven approximately 45 minutes, or until golden brown. Serve with mild salsa.

Victorian Garden Bed & Breakfast

1720-16th Street, Monroe, WI 53566
608-328-1720

Hosts: Jane and Pete Kessenich

The Victorian Garden has been welcoming new and old friends since Spring 1990. The house is a comfortable, yet graceful home, filled with personal collections. We open our doors with a smile and extend a hand of friendship. Backyard gardens, wrap-around porch, and the front porch church pew all beckon you to come enjoy the surroundings. We offer healthy breakfasts, attention to detail, but most of all a comfortable place to step back in time to relax.

*Rates at the Victorian Garden Bed & Breakfast range from $40–$75.
Rates include a full breakfast.*

Sun-dried Tomato/Cheese Frittata

I adapted this recipe from several sources and made it work for my particular need. The Monroe area produces the only domestic Gruyere cheese made in the U.S., so I try to incorporate it into many of my dishes. This can be a low cholesterol dish by substituting Egg Beaters and a low-fat farmer cheese, or by substituting sauteed vegetables (zucchini, onion, mushrooms) for cheese. I like using the individual ramekins, placing them on dinner plates and surrounding it with sausage or Canadian bacon and a croissant. Nasturtiums or pansies nestled in lemon balm or mint make a lovely garnish.

serves 6-8

10-12	eggs
1/4	cup whole wheat bread crumbs
2	sun-dried tomatoes; julienned and then sliced in half *
1 1/2	cups shredded Gruyere cheese
	Several dashes Tabasco and Worcestershire sauce
1	teaspoon minced fresh basil leaves and chives

Preheat oven to 350 degrees. Spray individual ramekin dishes or 9-inch quiche pan with non-stick cooking spray.

Break eggs into a large bowl. Whip eggs to mix. Add bread crumbs, sun-dried tomatoes, cheese, and seasonings. If you wish, cover and refrigerate overnight.

Place mixture in ramekins or quiche pan. Bake 20 minutes for 4-inch ramekins or 35-45 minutes for large quiche pan. These puff up beautifully when done, so serve right from the oven.

*I prefer to use sun-dried tomatoes that are soaked in olive oil. If not available, use sun-dried tomatoes that are "reconstituted" by soaking in hot water for 10-15 minutes. Then cut into tiny pieces.

The Inn Bed & Breakfast

104 Wisconsin Avenue, Montreal, WI 54550
715-561-5180

Hosts: Doree and Dick Schumacher

The Inn is part of a former company town which is now on the National Register of Historic Places. The building, built in 1913, served as the office of Oglebay-Norton Iron Mining Co. The 4,335-foot-deep mine is the deepest in the world.

Iron County Heritage Area offers four season recreation including alpine and cross-country skiing, snowmobiling, biking, fishing, hiking, golfing, hunting, sailing, and canoeing. Take a break and enjoy the beautiful waterfall too.

Stenciling, antiques, and crocheted and hand-quilted bedspreads adorn the two-room suites. The walls of the third floor loft display memorabilia from the mining past. Relax and renew in a Finnish sauna. All units have private baths.

Rates at The Inn Bed & Breakfast range from $50-$70.
Rates include a full breakfast.

Honey Buns

These are for those days when you are sooo tired and the unexpected appear at the front door! This recipe is one you can mix together with ingredients you have on the shelf. It is relatively quick and easy. It is good for breakfast or afternoon tea. Vary the size of the buns, if you like, by using muffin tins of desired size and adjusting the baking time. One time I was out of pecans and used chopped dates. Good, too! Be sure to check buns after about 15 minutes so bottoms (actually tops to be) don't burn.

makes 8-12 buns

6	tablespoons butter, divided
1/3	cup honey
1/2	cup very finely chopped pecans
1/4	cup plus 2 tablespoons sugar, divided
2	cups biscuit mix
2/3	cup milk
1	teaspoon cinnamon

Mix 4 tablespoons butter with honey. Melt and spread in the bottom of 12 greased muffin tins. Sprinkle each with chopped pecans.

Add 2 tablespoons sugar to biscuit mix. Mix in milk. Roll dough out on floured board to 9x12-inch rectangle. Melt remaining butter and brush over dough. Sprinkle with mixture of remaining sugar and cinnamon. Roll up like jelly roll. Cut into 12 slices.

Place in muffin tins on top of honey-pecan mixture. Bake at 425 degrees for about 20 minutes.

Timm's Hill Bed & Breakfast

N2036 County Road C, Ogema, WI 54459
715-767-5288

Hosts: Joyce and Jim Summers

Our turn-of-the-century farmhouse is nestled in the hills surrounding Wisconsin's highest point, Timm's Hill. Climb the observation tower for a panoramic view of wooded hills and sparkling lakes. Autumn brings a spectacular show of colors.

Hike or bike the Timm's Hill Trail, an extension of the National Ice Age Trail, as it winds through hardwood forests. Ski groomed trails in winter.

Relax in country comfort in one of our three charming guest rooms. The Violet Room is a favorite for honeymoons or wedding anniversaries.

Wake up to the tantalizing smells of a hearty country breakfast.

Rates at the Timm's Hill Bed & Breakfast range from $50–$55. Rates include a full breakfast.

Timm's Hill Quiche

This quiche can be made with turkey ham if you are avoiding red meat. The meat can also be left out for a vegetarian-style quiche. Our guests love the aroma as it bakes.

serves 4

1	9-inch deep dish pie shell	3	tablespoons grated Parmesan cheese
1½	cups shredded Monterey Jack cheese	2	teaspoons chopped chives, optional
¼	cup diced green pepper	⅛	teaspoon cayenne pepper
¼	cup diced onion		Dash salt
½	cup sliced fresh mushrooms	5	eggs
½	cup diced ham or 6 slices lean bacon, fried and crumbled	1¼	cups half-and-half

Preheat oven to 350 degrees. Prick pie shell several times with fork. Bake 7-8 minutes until lightly browned. Reduce oven heat to 325 degrees.

Line bottom of pie shell with half of the Monterey Jack cheese. In medium bowl, mix green pepper, onion, mushrooms, and ham. Sprinkle over cheese. Top with remaining Monterey Jack cheese.

Combine Parmesan cheese, chives, cayenne pepper, salt, eggs, and half-and-half. Mix well. Pour over ingredients in pie shell.

Bake at 325 degrees about 1 hour 15 minutes or until firm and lightly browned on top. Remove from oven and cool slightly before cutting.

Pleasant Lake Inn Bed & Breakfast

2238-60th Avenue, Osceola, WI 54020-4509
715-294-2545, 1-800-294-2545

Hosts: Richard and Charlene Berg

Each of our guest rooms is history-filled—from poems and possessions from a great-grandfather who settled our still-operating dairy farm in 1857, to information about and the wedding dress of a great-grandmother who was the first white girl born in St. Paul, Minnesota.

Relax in a spacious room or luxury suite with double whirlpools, around a crackling bonfire, or on your private deck or sun room. Take a leisurely walk in the woods or enjoy the lake in the canoe or paddle boat.

Pleasant Lake Inn is also near antique shops, golf, state park, cross-country ski trails, bike trails, and rivers to canoe.

Rates at the Pleasant Lake Inn Bed & Breakfast range from $55-$100.
Rates include a full breakfast.

Honey Puffed Pancake

*Many years ago, I found this recipe in a farm magazine
and thought it would be something my family would like.
It's quick and easy too. This is a favorite with the guests,
especially with the Honey Butter Spread. I use half fresh
stone-ground whole wheat flour and half all-purpose flour
to add nutrition and great taste to this pancake.*

serves 6

1 cup milk	Honey Butter Spread:
6 eggs	1/2 cup honey
3 tablespoons honey	1/2 cup powdered sugar
3 ounces cream cheese, softened	1/2 cup butter, softened
1 cup flour	Cinnamon to taste
1/2 teaspoon salt	
1/2 teaspoon baking powder	
3 tablespoons butter, divided	

Preheat oven to 400 degrees.

In blender, put milk, eggs, honey, cream cheese, flour, salt, and baking powder. Blend ingredients in blender at high speed for 1 minute or until smooth.

Grease 10-inch ovenproof skillet with 1 tablespoon butter. Add remaining 2 tablespoons butter. Heat skillet in oven until butter sizzles. Pour batter into heated skillet and bake for 20-25 minutes or until puffed and golden brown. Pancake will flatten to about 1 inch after being removed from oven.

While pancake is baking, make spread. Beat honey, powdered sugar, butter, and cinnamon together until well mixed.

Serve pancake with Honey Butter Spread and syrup, if desired.

A Summer Place

106 Main Street, Pepin, WI 54759
715-442-2132

Hostess: Mary Lou Devlin

Enjoy a touch of Cape Cod overlooking beautiful Lake Pepin. Imagine white-washed wood, wicker, a picket fence, a marvelous array of brightly colored flowers, and the clanking of sailboat halyard lines.

A Summer Place, open Thursday through Monday, May through October, offers three unique bedrooms, each with a full bath, two-person whirlpool, and a large common deck off the guest sitting area with a spectacular view of Pepin Harbor.

During your stay, enjoy sailing, depending on the weather and captain's availability; experience excellent dining at Pepin's Harbor View Cafe, one of Wisconsin's best restaurants, located right across the street; and tour the birthplace of Laura Ingalls Wilder.

Rates at A Summer Place range from $65–$95.
Rates include a continental breakfast.

Bananas Exceptional

*This is a unique and very simple fruit dish
which is especially nice to use when fresh berries
are not available.*

serves 4

4	bananas
1/2	cup sour cream
1/2	cup cream
1	teaspoon cinnamon
4	tablespoons brown sugar

Slice bananas and place in 4 individual serving dishes.

In small bowl, mix together sour cream and cream. Spoon equal amounts over bananas in serving dishes. In another small bowl, mix together cinnamon and brown sugar. Sprinkle equal amounts over cream. Serve.

The Kraemer House
Bed & Breakfast

1190 Spruce Street, Plain, WI 53577
608-546-3161

Hosts: Gwen and Duane Kraemer

The Kraemer House Bed & Breakfast is located in a quaint and very progressive village. The area has lots of Indian history. All the Indian tribes met on a hill overlooking the valley where Plain is now located. The hill, which is now called St. Anne's Hill, was called Council Bluff by all the Indian tribes that met there.

In Plain you can watch cheese making and purchase cheese at Cedar Grove cheese factory. Spring Green, just seven miles away, offers the famous American Players Theater, Frank Lloyd Wright's Talisien, and The House On the Rock.

At The Kraemer House you are treated with very special care: robes in the rooms, early morning coffee right outside your door, a welcome home turn-down service, and a different full breakfast every morning.

Rates at The Kraemer House Bed & Breakfast range from $50-$85. Rates include a full breakfast.

Raspberry Coffee Cake

This recipe was given to me 30-some years ago by a friend, and I have made it every year since. I guess this coffee cake has become kind of my specialty. I make this cake at least eight to ten times while my raspberries are in season and use only fresh berries, not frozen. That's why it's so good and such a treat in the summer. This cake is best served the day it is made, although everyone else says it is just as good or better the next day. With the leftover egg whites, I always make a couple of angel food cakes.

serves 12-16

4	tablespoons butter		2	teaspoons vanilla extract
3	egg yolks		2	cups red raspberries
1	cup sugar			Butter Cream Frosting:
2	cups flour		2	teaspoons butter
1/4	teaspoon salt		1 1/2	cups powdered sugar
2	teaspoons baking powder		1-2	tablespoons milk
1	cup milk		1	teaspoon vanilla extract

Cream together butter, egg yolks, and sugar until very creamy. In separate bowl, sift together flour, salt, and baking powder. Add milk and flour alternately to butter; mix well. Add vanilla and mix thoroughly. Pour batter into greased and floured 9x13-inch pan.

Wash and drain raspberries well; place on top of batter. Bake cake at 350 degrees 25-30 minutes, or until a wooden pick inserted in center comes out clean.

To make frosting, mix together butter, powdered sugar, milk, and vanilla until very creamy. This will be a very small amount of frosting.

Cool cake 10-15 minutes; then spread frosting over top of warm cake.

Johnson Inn

231 West North Street, P.O. Box 487, Plainfield, WI 54966
715-335-4383

Proprietors: Roger and Lois Johnson
Hosts: Burrell and Nancy Johnson

We at the Johnson Inn welcome you to "Wake up in the Past." Our newly and carefully restored 1800's home has manicured grounds and colorful flower beds; two fireplaces; two open stairways; and four lovely guest rooms with Amish quilts on the beds.

Antiquing, downhill and cross-country skiing, snowmobiling, fishing, biking, hunting, and much more is right outside our door.

We invite you to join us and leave your worries on the doorstep.

Rates at the Johnson Inn range from $40-$75.
Rates include a full breakfast.

Apple Glazed Sausages

*The onions seem to absorb any remaining grease from the
sausages, leaving a lean and apple-tasting link.
These flavorful sausages make a nice side dish
with eggs and waffles.*

serves 6-8

1	24-ounce package regular sausage links, fresh or frozen
2/3	cup water
1/2	cup packed brown sugar, light or dark
4	large tart apples, peeled and cored, then sliced
2	large onions, sliced

Brown sausages in large skillet. Remove sausages, drain on paper
towels, and wash skillet or use clean one. Add water, brown sugar, apples,
onions, and sausages to skillet. Simmer on low heat for 20-30 minutes,
just until sausages are nicely coated with brown sugar. Stir occasionally
to prevent burning. Serve sausages hot with egg main dish, discarding
apples and onions.

Yankee Hill Inn Bed & Breakfast

405 Collins Street, Plymouth, WI 53073
414-892-2222

Hosts: Peg and Jim Stahlman

Named "One of Wisconsin's finest Inns and B&Bs"—
Wisconsin Trails magazine, June, 1994. We welcome you
into the ambiance of quiet, small town life in the heart of
the scenic Northern Kettle Moraine recreational area. We offer two
beautifully restored, award-winning, landmarked historic homes. One
is an 1891 Queen Anne home, which is a Sheboygan County
Landmark. The other, an 1870 Gothic Italianate, is listed on the
National Register of Historic Places.

It's a short, scenic drive to Wade House, Kettle Moraine recreational area, Road America, Black Wolf Run Golf Course, Kohler
Design Center, Woodlake Shops, and the Old Plank Road recreational
trail. You'll enjoy a stroll along the Mullet River to Hub City Antique
Mall and several excellent restaurants in downtown Plymouth.

Choose one of our 12 guest rooms all with private baths, including
six with whirlpool tubs. Gift certificates available in any denomination!

Rates at Yankee Hill Inn Bed & Breakfast range from $72-$96.
Rates include a full breakfast.

Applesauce Oatmeal Muffins

*You'll love the aroma
radiating from your kitchen as these muffins bake.
They certainly set the stage for the breakfast to follow!*

makes 15 muffins

---

1 1/2	cups dry oatmeal, quick or old fashioned	3	tablespoons vegetable oil
1 1/4	cups all-purpose flour	1	egg white
3/4	teaspoon cinnamon		
1	teaspoon baking powder		**Topping:**
3/4	teaspoon baking soda	1/4	cup dry oatmeal
1	cup unsweetened applesauce	1	tablespoon brown sugar
1/2	cup skim milk	1/8	teaspoon cinnamon
1/2	cup brown sugar, firmly packed	1	tablespoon margarine, melted

In large bowl, combine oatmeal, flour, cinnamon, baking powder, and baking soda. Add applesauce, milk, brown sugar, oil, and egg white; mix until dry ingredients are just moistened. Fill muffin cups almost full.

In small bowl, combine topping ingredients; sprinkle evenly over batter.

Bake in 400-degree oven 20-22 minutes, or until deep golden brown.

Port Washington Inn

308 West Washington Street, Port Washington, WI 53074
414-284-5583

Hosts: Connie and Craig Siwy

*P*ampering guests is our specialty, and our 1903 Victorian provides the atmosphere in which to be pampered. Guests are amazed that the original Lincrusta wall coverings still remain in the home's entryway and main parlor. Original gas and electric light fixtures, stained glass, and polished oak adorn the house as well.

Guests awaken to the aroma of fresh-brewed coffee on a tea tray outside their rooms one hour before breakfast—just in time to smell the homemade muffins or coffeecake and hash brown casserole baking.

We're five blocks from Lake Michigan and within walking distance of many excellent restaurants and shops.

Rates at the Port Washington Inn range from $60–$95.
Rates include a full breakfast.

Strawberry Stuffed French Toast

*I love to hear the "mmm's" from the dining room
when guests take their first bite of this French toast.
In winter, I substitute chopped pecans for strawberries—
guests love it both ways.*

serves 8

1	8-ounce package cream cheese, softened
2	teaspoons vanilla extract
4	tablespoons sugar, divided
4-6	strawberries, diced
2	loaves white, unsliced old-fashioned-type bread or egg twist bread
6	eggs
1/2	cup milk
	Butter flavored shortening or non-stick cooking spray

Combine cream cheese, vanilla, 2 tablespoons sugar, and strawberries and mix well. Slice bread into sixteen 1½-inch slices (two per person). Slice a pocket in the center of each from the top to within ¼ inch of the bottom of each slice. Spread about 1 tablespoon cream cheese mixture in each pocket.

Mix eggs, milk, and remaining sugar. Dip bread slices in egg mixture and let pieces soak on a cookie sheet in the refrigerator for 1 hour. Fry on a griddle in a little shortening until both sides are golden brown. Serve with maple syrup.

Breese Waye Bed & Breakfast

816 MacFarlane Road, Portage, WI 53901
608-742-5281

Hosts: Keith and Gretchen Sprecher

Like a visit to Grandma's house. Built in 1880 by Llywelyn Breese, one of the founding fathers of Portage, this home has remained one of the more stately in the area. Noted for its elegance, each guest room is large and furnished with antiques.

Portage is a hub of historic, scenic, and recreational entertainment.

Rates at the Breese Way Bed & Breakfast range from $50–$70.
Rates include a full breakfast.

Breakfast Banana Split

*This quick dish is ideal for summer when berries and fruit
are in season. Use a variety of fruits to make the servings
colorful; green grapes, strawberries, and oranges go well.*

serves 4

4   bananas
2   cups each of 3 chopped fruits of your choice
     Hot fudge sauce
     Caramel sauce
     Crushed nuts, garnish
     Coconut, garnish

Slice bananas into bite-size pieces and place along outer edges of 4
banana split dishes. Place 1 ice-cream scoop (about 1/2 cup) of each fruit
on top of bananas in each dish.

Drizzle chocolate or caramel sauce over fruit and garnish with nuts
and coconuts.

Jamieson House Inn

407 North Franklin, P.O. Box 237, Poynette, WI 53955
608-635-4100

Hostess: Heidi Hutchison

*I*n 1878 Hugh Jamieson, a Scottish immigrant, was determined "to build a good substantial home and surround it with such conveniences as might afford some comfort and consolation for the many years of hard and incessant toil" he had passed through.

Now, the Jamieson House Inn, three dignified brick homes, make this not just the perfect place for a weekend getaway but also an ideal location for retreats, small conferences, meetings, and receptions.

The restaurant on the lower level, "Emily's European Cafe," is reminiscent of a fine rural German restaurant and offers a menu specializing in savory dishes of European origin.

Rates at the Jamieson House Inn range from $65–$130. Rates include a full breakfast.

Devonshire Cream

During the summer season, when fresh berries are abundantly available, there is nothing more delightful at breakfast than a small bowl filled with these tasty, colorful jewels topped with Devonshire Cream.

serves 8

1	cup heavy cream
1/2	cup sugar
1/4	teaspoon vanilla extract
1/2	teaspoon Creme de Cassis
3	tablespoons cold water
3/4	teaspoon gelatin
1	cup sour half-and-half

In a mixing bowl, combine heavy cream, sugar, vanilla extract, and Creme de Cassis and whip at high speed until a "soft peak" consistency is reached.

In a small saucepan, add cold water to gelatin and stir until gelatin is dispersed. Heat the mixture to about 125 degrees—the solution will be clear.

While heating the gelatin mixture, put sour half-and-half in a separate bowl. Immediately stir hot gelatin mixture into sour half-and-half until completely blended.

Add sour half-and-half mixture to whipped cream and blend at low speed until the mixture is smooth and creamy. ENJOY!!

Parkview Bed & Breakfast

211 North Park Street, Reedsburg, WI 53959
608-524-4333

Hosts: Tom and Donna Hofmann

Our 1895 home was built by a person who had a hardware business in Reedsburg. The original hardware is still in the home that also boasts leaded and etched glass windows, a suitor's window, beautiful woodwork, tray ceilings, and other unique features. The second owner of the home left a legacy of stones and shell ponds and lawn ornaments outside. Guests enjoy the flower and water gardens and fish in the two ponds.

Donna, a home economist, enjoys preparing the homemade breakfasts suited to guests. She uses foods in season and is always searching for and trying new recipes.

Parkview is centrally located for Wisconsin Dells, Baraboo, and Spring Green attractions. Guests enjoy using the newly opened 400-mile recreational trail that begins in Reedsburg.

Rates at the Parkview Bed & Breakfast range from $55-$70.
Rates include a full breakfast.

Large Breakfast Pancake

*Many years before opening our bed and breakfast,
Donna found this basic recipe and has adapted it over the
years. It is a favorite of our family and guests. By changing
the topping on the puffy pancake, it can easily change with
the season of fruits available. At Parkview Bed & Breakfast,
Donna makes her own topping from fruits, such as cherries,
berries, peaches, nectarines, apples, or combination of fruits,
which she sweetens and thickens.*

serves 2-4

2	tablespoons butter or margarine
1/2	cup flour
1/4	teaspoon salt
1	tablespoon sugar
1/2	cup milk
3	eggs

Topping:
2   tablespoons lemon juice
2   tablespoons powdered sugar
    or any prepared pie filling

Heat oven to 425 degrees. Melt butter in 9-10-inch ovenproof skillet or pie pan in oven until butter sizzles, about 2-5 minutes. Meanwhile, in a medium bowl, combine flour, salt, sugar, milk, and eggs. Beat with mixer. Tilt pie pan to coat bottom and sides with melted butter. Pour pancake batter into hot pan.

Bake for 14-18 minutes or until puffed and golden brown (it will be puffed up, especially on the sides). After taking from oven, remove to serving plate if desired. Sprinkle with lemon juice and then with powdered sugar or with fruit topping. Cut into wedges and serve.

Lamb's Inn Bed & Breakfast

Route 2 Box 144, Richland Center, WI 53581
608-585-4301

Hosts: Dick and Donna Messerschmidt

Relax on our 180-acre farm located in a quiet valley with wildlife and spectacular scenery. On our property, guests enjoy the large spring with trout and woods for hiking. At the bed and breakfast, relax on the porch, in the library, or in one of the four bedrooms with private baths, all of which are completely renovated.

Sitting across the road, high on the hill, is a new private cottage. Every window frames a beautiful view. This fully-equipped cottage has a queen-size bed, a spiral staircase leading to the loft with twin beds, and a deck for relaxing.

Nearby attractions include Taliesin, House on the Rock, American Players Theater, and Elroy-Sparta Bike Trail.

Rates at the Lamb's Inn Bed & Breakfast range from $70-$105.
Rates include a full breakfast in the inn
and a continental breakfast at the cottage.

Italian Vegetable Quiche

serves 6

_____ _____

1	9-inch deep dish pastry shell	1	cup shredded cheddar cheese
6	eggs	1	cup shredded mozzarella cheese
3/4	cup sour cream	1 1/2	cups milk
2	tablespoons butter	1	cup diced fresh tomatoes
1/3	cup chopped onion	1	teaspoon basil
8	ounces sliced fresh mushrooms	1	teaspoon salt

Preheat oven to 350 degrees. Prebake pastry shell 10 minutes.

In large bowl, beat eggs and add sour cream.

Heat butter in small skillet over medium-high heat. Saute onions 1-2 minutes, then add mushrooms. Saute until onions are translucent and mushrooms are softened.

Add onion, mushrooms, cheeses, milk, tomatoes, basil, and salt to eggs; mix well. Pour into pastry shell. Bake 45 minutes or until a knife inserted into the middle comes out clean.

Knollwood House Bed & Breakfast

N8257-950th St. Knollwood Drive, River Falls, WI 54022
715-425-1040, 1-800-435-0628

Hosts: Jim and Judy Tostrud

Guests at the Knollwood House always mention how peaceful and relaxing it is. The fresh country air helps them to rest well in the comfortable and cozy guest rooms. Relaxing in the hammock or yard swing amidst the beautiful flower gardens and fish ponds adds to their pleasure.

For those wanting a little more activity, the outdoor pool, sauna, hot tub, golf green (3 tees), hiking/cross-country/snowshoe trails are on the property plus many scenic and rustic roads for bicycling are nearby. The Kinnickinnic River, a class I trout stream, flows through River Falls. Small helicopters can land on the property, while others wishing to fly in can use the city airport just across the field. Breakfasts are served when guests want them and are delicious.

Rates at Knollwood House Bed & Breakfast range from $80–$95.
Rates include a full breakfast.

Rhubarb Muffins

One morning, a friend came for coffee
and had the recipe for these muffins attached to the basket.
A good rhubarb muffin recipe must be hard to find as most
of our guests who are served these muffins ask for the recipe.
They are easy to prepare, freeze well, and travel well.

makes 15 medium muffins

1¼	cups brown sugar, packed	Topping:
½	cup oil	1 tablespoon butter
1	egg	½ cup sugar
2	teaspoons vanilla extract	1 teaspoon cinnamon
1	cup buttermilk	1½ tablespoons nuts, optional
1½	cups rhubarb	
1½	cups chopped nuts, optional	
2½	cups flour	
1	teaspoon baking soda	
1	teaspoon baking powder	
½	teaspoon salt	

In large mixer bowl, beat together brown sugar, oil, egg, vanilla, buttermilk, and rhubarb until well blended. Add nuts.

In small bowl, mix together flour, baking soda, baking powder, and salt. Combine wet and dry mixtures and stir until blended.

Fill greased muffin tins two-thirds full. In small bowl, mix together butter, sugar, cinnamon, and nuts for topping. Sprinkle over muffins. Bake at 350 degrees for 20 minutes.

The Wooden Heart Inn

11086 Hwy 42, Sister Bay, WI 54234
414-854-9097

Hosts: Marilyn and Mike Hagerman

We welcome you to our newly-constructed log home nestled in the woods on the north side of Sister Bay in Door County, Wisconsin. It combines the charm of an old home with modern amenities and is furnished with meticulously restored antiques. Our guests are welcome to use our front porch with its old-fashioned swing and rocking chairs, the great room with its large fieldstone fireplace, or the deck and gazebo in the rear of the house.

Guests are served a full country breakfast on a 180-piece set of hand-painted Bavarian china dated from 1890. The three guest rooms are located on the second floor along with a loft where guests may watch TV, play games, or read. Each room has a queen-sized bed and a small private bath with shower. The rooms are decorated in themes—apples, cherries, and hearts. There is a gift shop, located off the great room—called "The Back Porch"—specializing in bird houses, bird feeders, and other bird-related items.

One of our guests wrote to us, "The Wooden Heart Inn is a very welcome addition to the world of bed and breakfasts. We give a four-heart rating to your inn."

Rates at The Wooden Heart Inn range from $80–$90.
Rates include a full breakfast.

Stuffed French Toast
with Blueberry Sauce

*We like this recipe because it can be made the night before.
We garnish the plate with an orange slice, a slice of kiwi,
and a sprig of fresh mint from our garden.
We also serve it with sausage or bacon.*

serves 6-8

16	slices white bread	Blueberry Sauce:	
1	8-ounce package neufachatel cream cheese	1	orange
10	eggs	2	cups blueberries, fresh or frozen, thawed
1/3	cup maple syrup	1	cup sugar
2	cups milk		Dash nutmeg

Grease a 9x13-inch baking pan. Remove and discard crust from the bread; cut remaining bread into 1/2-inch cubes. Cut cheese into 1/2-inch cubes. Layer half of bread in pan. Next add cheese, then the remainder of the bread. Beat eggs and mix with maple syrup and milk. Pour egg mixture over bread and cheese. Cover and refrigerate overnight.

Bake at 375 degrees, covered, for 15 minutes. Remove cover and bake an additional 30 minutes.

Cut into squares and serve with blueberry sauce.

To prepare blueberry sauce, grate peel from orange and squeeze juice; place in a medium saucepan. Mix blueberries, sugar, and nutmeg together and add to saucepan. Bring to a boil, then cook on low heat for 5 minutes. Sauce can be made ahead of time, then served warm or cold.

Just-N-Trails Bed & Breakfast/ Nordic Ski Center

Route 1 Box 274, Sparta, WI 54656
608-269-4522, 1-800-488-4521

Hosts: Don and Donna Justin

We specialize in Recreation—groomed cross-country ski trails, famous Elroy-Sparta Bike Trail, hiking, canoeing; Relaxation—two-acre landscaped lawn and gardens located in a private valley, cuddle the numerous teddy bears; Romance— soak in a whirlpool bath, dream by the fireplace, make plans in an authentic Scandinavian-scribed log cabin with a log bed. Experience education or nostalgia on a working dairy farm. We welcome all ages and offer plenty of space for family reunions or meetings.

Rates at the Just-N-Trails Bed & Breakfast range from $70-$250. Rates include a full breakfast.

Cranberry Coffee Cake

Cranberries are Wisconsin's number one fruit crop.
Many of the colorful berries are grown in our county.
Therefore, they are frequently served to our guests.
This cranberry coffee cake is light, moist
and melts in your mouth.

serves 10

3/4	cup vegetable oil	3/4	teaspoon salt
1	cup sugar	1 1/2	cups plain non-fat yogurt
3	eggs	1 1/2	cups cranberries, fresh and
1	teaspoon almond extract		chopped or dried
3	cups flour		
2	teaspoons baking powder		Glaze:
1	teaspoon baking soda	1	cup powdered sugar
		2	tablespoons orange juice
		1	teaspoon almond extract

In large bowl, cream oil and sugar until light and fluffy. Add eggs, one at a time, beating thoroughly after each addition. Beat in almond extract.

In medium bowl, sift together flour, baking powder, baking soda, and salt. Add dry ingredients to creamed mixture alternately with yogurt, beating well after each addition.

Preheat oven to 350 degrees. Spray 9x13-inch glass baking pan with cooking spray. Spoon half of the batter into pan. Sprinkle cranberries over batter. Cover with remaining batter. Bake 1 hour.

To make glaze, mix powdered sugar, orange juice, and almond extract together until smooth. Spread over baked coffee cake while still warm.

The Lodge at River's Edge

HC 2 Box 244-6, Spread Eagle, WI 54121
715-696-3406

Hosts: John and Carol Moldenhauer

We invite you to come and "share the quiet" of our elegant new home, secluded amid giant pines and hardwoods, in Spread Eagle, Wisconsin. "The Lodge" overlooks the Menominee River, the boundary water between northeastern Wisconsin and Michigan's Upper Peninsula, and is home, as well, to bald eagles, wild turkey, deer, and a rainbow of birds and waterfowl.

Our breakfasts are a culinary delight and are sometimes served aboard our pontoon boat while a river cruise is in progress—an adventure especially enjoyed by our guests.

Does the thought of canoeing our undisturbed rivers, snowshoeing into breathtaking waterfalls, hiking in state forests, biking the byways, skiing our mountains, snowmobiling into pristine country on groomed trails, or just lounging on the deck, dock, or fireside appeal to you? Then come share the beauty of this special place, whatever the season, and enjoy our special brand of pampering. "We are a bit out of the way but way out of the ordinary."

Rates at The Lodge at River's Edge range from $60–$75.
Rates include a full breakfast.

Divine Buttermilk Hot Cakes with Orange Syrup

The combination of feathery light hot cakes, studded with plump blueberries, and topped with tangy orange syrup brings raves from our guests and requests for "more." We also include homemade maple syrup (produced by our neighbors) for a syrup choice as well.

serves 6

1²/₃	cups flour	
1	tablespoon baking powder	
1¹/₂	teaspoons baking soda	
1	teaspoon salt	
2	tablespoons sugar	
2	cups buttermilk	
3	eggs, beaten	
3	tablespoons butter or margarine, melted and cooled	
1¹/₂	cups blueberries, fresh or frozen, optional	

Orange Syrup:

1¹/₂	cups orange juice, fresh preferred
2	tablespoons cornstarch
1	cup sugar
1/4	cup butter or margarine
4	teaspoons lemon juice, fresh preferred
2	teaspoons grated orange peel

Sift flour, baking powder, baking soda, salt, and sugar into large bowl. In a separate bowl combine buttermilk, eggs, and butter; stir to blend. Add to dry ingredients and mix lightly. Cook on a greased or non-stick hot griddle, using 1/4 cup batter per pancake. If desired, sprinkle blueberries over pancakes prior to turning to cook top side.

To make orange syrup, stir orange juice and cornstarch in small pan until smooth. Add sugar and stir over medium heat until thick and clear, 5-8 minutes. Add butter, lemon juice, and orange peel and stir until butter melts. Cool to warm and serve over pancakes.

Hill Street Bed & Breakfast

353 West Hill Street, Spring Green, WI 53588
608-588-7751

Hosts: Kelly and Jay Phelps

We welcome you to our 1900 Queen Anne Victorian home, with hand-crafted woodwork, two living rooms, and a newly remodeled lower level. Guests can browse through the towns' shops, art galleries, explore The House on the Rock, and Tower Hill State Park adjoining the Wisconsin River. A visit would not be complete without seeing architect Frank Lloyd Wright's Taliesin. Additionally, the American Players Theater presents the finest in classical theater. Recreational activities such as canoeing, championship golf, bicycling, and cross-country skiing are also readily available.

Rates at the Hill Street Bed & Breakfast range from $65–$75. Rates include a full breakfast.

Cappuccino Chip Muffins

These muffins are quick and easy to prepare.
Our guests request this recipe frequently.

makes 22 mini-muffins

2	cups flour
1/2	cup sugar
2 1/2	teaspoons baking powder
3	tablespoons French Roast instant coffee
1/2	teaspoon salt
1	cup milk
1/2	cup butter, melted
1	egg, beaten
1	teaspoon vanilla extract
1/2	cup mini-chocolate chips

Grease 22 mini-muffin tin cups. Preheat oven to 375 degrees.

In large bowl, stir together flour, sugar, baking powder, instant coffee, and salt. In another bowl, whisk together milk, butter, egg, and vanilla. Add to dry ingredients. Mix until just combined. Do not overmix. Add mini-chocolate chips.

Scoop batter into mini-muffin cups. Bake 15 minutes.

Dreams of Yesteryear
Bed & Breakfast

1100 Brawley Street, Stevens Point, WI 54481
715-341-4525

Hosts: Bonnie and Bill Maher

This elegant turn-of-the-century Victorian Queen Anne home is listed on the National Register of Historic Places and was featured in *Victorian Homes* magazine. Dreams offers four guest rooms on three floors, incorporating historic ambiance with today's lifestyle. Private baths, private reading rooms, and a whirlpool tub are just a few amenities we have to offer. We are originally from Stevens Point and enjoy sharing the history of our house, our antique furnishings, and our community.

We're located three blocks from historic downtown Stevens Point. Come visit Dreams of Yesteryear. "It's the kind of place Victorian dreams are made of."

Rates at the Dreams of Yesteryear Bed & Breakfast range from $55–$125. Rates include a full breakfast.

Dutch Apple Roll

*This recipe is adapted from an old recipe my grandmother
used. It makes a nice basis around which to build a special
breakfast for family or guests. Serve with sausage links and
a good French roast coffee for a flavorful fall country
breakfast or serve with glazed ham and your favorite
gourmet coffee for more formal occasions.*

serves 8-12

6	medium apples		Syrup:	
2	cups flour		2	cups sugar
1	teaspoon salt		2	cups water
2	teaspoons baking powder		1/4	teaspoon cinnamon
3/4	cup shortening		1/4	cup butter
1/2	cup milk			
3/4	cup sugar			
1	tablespoon cinnamon			

Prepare apples by peeling, coring, and chopping. Set aside.

In medium bowl, sift together flour, salt, and baking powder. Cut in shortening and add milk. Roll out on floured board to 1/4-inch thickness. Place chopped apples over dough. Sprinkle with sugar and cinnamon. Roll up as a jelly roll, cut in slices, and arrange in a 9x13-inch baking pan. Roll of dough may instead be wrapped in foil and frozen to be sliced and baked later.

Make syrup by dissolving sugar in water and boiling in saucepan. Add cinnamon and butter and boil until slightly thickened. Pour syrup over apple roll slices and bake in 375-degree oven for 25-35 minutes or until crust starts to turn golden brown.

Victorian Swan on Water

1716 Water Street, Stevens Point, WI 54481
715-345-0595

Hostess: Joan Ouellette

Happy memories never wear out. We specialize in happy memories–good food, good conversation, great atmosphere. Share in the history and comfort of this 1889 Victorian home. Summer fills the backyard with flowers, a splashing waterfall, and comfortable seating. In winter, get next to a cozy fireplace with a good book.

All the activities of Central Wisconsin are available to you. Miles of walking and bike paths, cross-country ski trails, golf courses, fishing, historic downtown, and lots of antique shops are just a few of the good times waiting for you.

Rates at the Victorian Swan on Water range from $55–$120.
Rates include a full breakfast.

Fabulous Noodle Kugel

*This recipe was in my box of things to try for 40 years.
One day I was desperate for something different,
and I really did like the funny name. Imagine my surprise
when a room full of guests cried "Noodle Kugel."
I had no idea it was an authentic Jewish dish.
This is a make ahead dish.*

serves 12

7	eggs	1/2	cup butter
1	cup sugar	1	pound broad egg noodles, cooked and kept warm
1	16-ounce container cottage cheese		Topping:
2	cups sour cream	1/4	cup crushed cornflakes
2	cups milk	2	teaspoons cinnamon
2	teaspoons vanilla extract	1/4	cup sugar
1	cup golden raisins		Sour cream for garnish, optional

Mix eggs and sugar. Add cottage cheese, sour cream, milk, vanilla, and raisins. In separate bowl, add butter to warm noodles, stirring until melted. Combine noodles with cottage cheese mixture. Pour into 9x13-inch glass pan. Refrigerate overnight.

Preheat oven to 350 degrees. To make topping, combine cornflakes, cinnamon, and sugar; sprinkle over top of kugel. Bake 1 hour. Let dish set for about 5 minutes before serving. Cut into squares and garnish with sour cream.

The Gray Goose Bed & Breakfast

4258 Bay Shore Drive, Sturgeon Bay, WI 54235
414-743-9100

Hosts: Jack and Jessie Burkhardt

Located out of, but close to, the city on a quiet, wooded site next to an apple orchard, The Gray Goose epitomizes the term "country," which is really what Door County always was, and what most visitors want it to remain.

This is one of the very few bed and breakfasts in the "Cape Cod of the Midwest" with a real view of woods and water. In the true tradition of bed and breakfast inns, you'll find warm, personal hospitality; a full, delicious, "skip-lunch" breakfast; seasonal snacks and beverages; plenty of space to just kick back and take it easy; shared baths; and hosts ready to help you in every way.

This is an 1862 home with the entire second floor made over especially for guests and furnished with authentic antiques. There are many windows for air, light, and just looking; four large rooms with luxurious bedding; a guest sitting room with games, piano, and cable TV; a full front porch with old wicker and a swing; and a strikingly beautiful dining room where guests breakfast together by candle, lamp, and sunlight at an 1874 table whose setting changes every day.

Rates at The Gray Goose Bed & Breakfast range from $65–$80.
Rates include a full breakfast.

Zucchini-Tomato Pie

*This is a great breakfast entree for any guests,
especially vegetarian guests. I make it the night before to
allow flavors to blend and to make the morning go smoother.
I usually serve a separate meat with this pie, preferably
bratwurst. To add a spark of flavor to the brats, fry them,
then simmer in 1/2 cup orange juice and 1 cup water
to just cover brats.*

serves 8

4	medium zucchini squash	4	large eggs (or a total of 4
1	medium onion		tablespoons egg substitute)
2	tablespoons butter	1/4	cup half-and-half
3	tablespoons vegetable oil	2	large tomatoes
1/2	teaspoon garlic salt	2	teaspoons grated Parmesan
1/4	teaspoon pepper		cheese
1	teaspoon oregano		

Slice zucchini in rounds 1/4- to 1/2-inch thick and saute until almost tender. Slice and chop onion; saute in butter and oil with garlic salt, pepper, and oregano until onions are tender.

Butter 10-inch round baking dish thoroughly. Put zucchini in baking dish and cover with onion mixture. Beat eggs and half-and-half and pour over onion layer. Arrange tomato slices to completely cover top. Sprinkle Parmesan cheese over tomatoes. Cover with plastic wrap and refrigerate overnight.

Bake uncovered in 350-degree oven for a maximum of 1 hour.

Hearthside Bed & Breakfast Inn

2136 Taube Road, Sturgeon Bay, WI 54235
414-746-2136

Hosts: Don and Louise Klussendorf

At Hearthside you will find... "warm hospitality" and "good old German traditions"...delicious wholesome full breakfast and snacks, well-kept rooms, comfortable queen-size and twin beds, TVs in each room, and private baths. Hearthside is located just a few minutes from the shops and activity of Sturgeon Bay. Herman Taube came to America in 1871 from Brennan, Germany. The house was built sometime in the 1880's for Herman's wife, Emilia, and their 12 children. The barn still stands nearby. We thank them for leaving us such a wonderful house to share with our guests.

Rates at the Hearthside Bed & Breakfast Inn range from $40-$50.
Rates include a full breakfast.

Popovers

*This was my family's
favorite Sunday morning breakfast.
Fill with jam or jelly and serve
with juice, fruit, coffee, or milk.*

makes 18 popovers

6	eggs
1½	cups milk
1½	tablespoons cooking oil
1½	cups flour
¾	teaspoon salt

Preheat oven to 400 degrees.

In large bowl, beat eggs well. Add milk and beat to combine. Beat in oil. Sift flour and salt slowly into liquid. Beat 2 more minutes.

Spoon into well-greased muffin tins. Bake for 25 minutes.

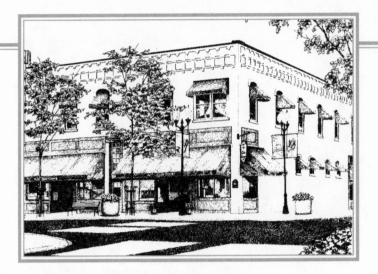

Inn at Cedar Crossing

336 Louisiana Street, Sturgeon Bay, WI 54235
414-743-4200

Hostess: Terry Wulf

Warm hospitality, elegant antique-filled guest rooms, and creative regional cuisine are tradition at this most intimate Door County inn, included on the National Register of Historic Places. Lovingly restored, you'll find cozy fireplaces, room service, and evening refreshments await pampered travellers. Guest rooms are exceptionally furnished—oversized canopied beds, double whirlpool tubs, private porches, and inviting fireplaces. Exquisite dining features fresh ingredients, enticingly prepared entrees, sinful desserts, scratch bakery, and casual pub set in the beauty and culture of Wisconsin's Door Peninsula.

Rates at the Inn at Cedar Crossing range from $79–$138.
Rates include a continental breakfast.

Dried Cherry and Almond Scones

*We enjoy utilizing the fruits of our local
orchard fruit growers in our recipes. Did you know we use
approximately five tons of Door County tart cherries in our
restaurant each year?*

makes 12 scones

5	cups flour	2	eggs
3/4	cup sugar	1	teaspoon almond extract
2	teaspoons salt		Milk
2	tablespoons baking powder		
1	cup sliced almonds		Egg Wash:
1	cup dried cherries	1	egg
	(Cherry De-Lite)	1/4	cup water
3/4	cup butter, softened		

Combine flour, sugar, salt, and baking powder in large mixer bowl. Add almonds and cherries. Stir until combined. Add softened butter and mix until incorporated.

Crack eggs into a 2-cup measure and add almond extract. Add milk to equal $1\frac{1}{2}$ cups total liquid. Add liquids, mixing on low until combined. The dough should be moist, not sticky.

Roll out dough about $1\frac{1}{4}$-inch thick on a floured surface. Using a 3-inch cutter, cut out scones and place on parchment paper or greased 12x18-inch pan. To make egg wash, add egg to water and whisk to combine. Brush top of scones with egg wash. Bake in 375-degree oven until golden brown and firm to the touch, about 25 minutes.

The Scofield House Bed & Breakfast

908 Michigan Street, P.O. Box 761, Sturgeon Bay, WI 54235
414-743-7727

Hosts: Bill and Fran Cecil

The Scofield House, considered by travel writers to be "The most elegant B & B in Door County," is an authentic turn-of-the century, restored 1902 Victorian bed and breakfast inn. The decor is "high Victorian" and all six guest rooms/suites are resplendent with fine antiques, private baths—many with double whirlpools, fireplaces, TV/VCR/stereo, and complimentary movie library. In 1992 the entire third floor "room at the top" suite was completed.

The Scofield House was discovered by Fran and Bill Cecil in 1987. They dropped their health care careers and bought and restored the house, teaching themselves the art of innkeeping. Now many years and several thousand guests later, the Scofield House has been featured in numerous magazines, books, and newspapers including *Midwest Living, Country Inns, Glamour, Wisconsin Trails, Victorian Decorating and Lifestyle,* and *Chicago Tribune.*

The Scofield House has always been "smoke free" and air-conditioned. A full gourmet breakfast, afternoon teas, and "sweet treats" are complimentary for guests.

Rates at the Scofield House range from $79-$189.
Rates include a full breakfast.

Bacon-Cheddar Baked Eggs

*This is a quick and easy to assemble breakfast dish.
Using custard cups or shirred egg dishes, the presentation
is attractive and easy to handle. We use this dish when
preparing more complicated fruit accompaniments and
muffins to give us extra time in between courses at breakfast.*

serves 8

16	slices bacon, cooked crisp and drained
	Butter or margarine, optional
16	extra large eggs
	Salt and pepper to taste
	Pinch chives
8	teaspoons fine dried bread crumbs
8	teaspoons milk
3/4-1	cup shredded cheddar cheese

Crumble cooked bacon. Brush individual baking dishes with butter or margarine. Crack 2 eggs into each baking dish. Sprinkle with salt, pepper, and chives. Sprinkle approximately 1/4 cup crumbled bacon over eggs in each dish and then sprinkle with 1 teaspoon bread crumbs. Pour 1 teaspoon milk over eggs, sprinkle with 1-2 tablespoons shredded cheddar cheese.

Bake at 350 degrees for 13-15 minutes or until eggs are set.

White Lace Inn

16 North 5th Avenue, Sturgeon Bay, WI 54235
414-743-1105

Hosts: Bonnie and Dennis Statz

White Lace Inn's three historic homes are clustered together in the midst of colorful perennial gardens, a white gazebo, and brick lined pathways, creating a welcoming atmosphere. When you enter the main house to check in, you're greeted with warm hospitality. Each of 15 guest rooms is wonderfully inviting and decorated in a cheerful mix of fabrics, lovely wallpapers, white linens, quality antiques, and of course, a gentle touch of lace. All guest rooms have a private bathroom and many feature a double whirlpool, fireplace or both. Our door is open every day of the year.

Rates at the White Lace Inn range from $68-$155.
Rates include a continental breakfast.

Bonnie's Lemon Blueberry Muffins

*We use fresh lemon balm from the herb garden
at the inn and sometimes add a tablespoon of chopped
lemon thyme also. These muffins are very moist
and flavorful—always a hit.*

makes 14-16 muffins

1/2	cup milk		Pinch salt	
	Grated zest of 1 lemon	2	tablespoons lemon juice
1	tablespoon lemon balm, optional	2	cups blueberries, fresh or frozen
6	tablespoons butter,		
	at room temperature	Glaze:
1	cup sugar	1	tablespoon fresh lemon juice
2	eggs, lightly beaten		(or more)
2	cups flour		Powdered sugar
2	teaspoons baking powder		

In a small saucepan, heat milk, then remove from heat. Add lemon zest and lemon balm; let cool. In large bowl, cream butter and add sugar gradually, beating until creamy. Add eggs slowly and beat well. In a separate large bowl, combine flour, baking powder, and salt. Add milk mixture to butter mixture; add lemon juice and mix well. Then add flour mixture and blend well. Add blueberries and stir gently until just combined. Fill paper-lined muffin cups at least 3/4 full.

Bake at 400 degrees 20-22 minutes. Be careful not to overbake. Muffins will be very light in color, not brown.

To make glaze, add powdered sugar to lemon juice until glaze is the consistency of a thin paste. While muffins are a little warm, drizzle with glaze.

Red Forest Bed & Breakfast

1421-25th Street, Two Rivers, WI 54241
414-793-1794

Hosts: Kay and Alan Rodewald

*T*he Family Rodewald warmly welcomes you to step back in time to 1907 and enjoy the Red Forest Bed & Breakfast. Red Forest is the English translation of our German name Rodewald. Our German heritage and old world charm is gently blended into our comfortable home, from the trophy deer mounts by the fireplace to Great-Grandparents' family wedding pictures in "Granny's Sewing Room" and the heirloom antiques throughout the house.

Two Rivers is a quiet little community where we specialize in RELAXATION…Comb the sugar-sand beaches, hike Point Beach State Park, or take a walk downtown in search of that special antique find. We're located midway between Chicago and the Door County Peninsula.

Rates at the Red Forest Bed & Breakfast range from $60-$75.
Rates include a full breakfast.

Maple Bran Muffins

*Muffins are made fresh daily at the Red Forest
and at check-out time, our guests are always sent on their
way with a small bag of leftover breakfast muffins.*

*Pure maple syrup, made locally by a family relative, is
always available and used regularly at the Red Forest.
There is just no comparison to the rich maple flavor
of the real thing!*

makes 12 muffins

3/4	cup natural wheat bran
1/2	cup milk
1/2	cup maple syrup
1	egg, lightly beaten
1/4	cup oil
11/4	cups whole wheat flour
3	teaspoons baking powder
1/2	teaspoon salt
1/3	cup chopped walnuts or pecans

Glaze:
1	tablespoon butter or margarine, softened
1/2	cup powdered sugar
1	tablespoon maple syrup

Combine bran, milk, and maple syrup in medium bowl. Mix in egg
and oil. Combine flour, baking powder, and salt and add to bran mixture
along with chopped walnuts or pecans. Stir just until moistened. Spoon
into greased or paper-lined muffin tins. Bake at 400 degrees for 18-20
minutes.

To prepare glaze, combine butter, sugar, and syrup in small bowl.
Stir to blend and spread over warm muffins.

Brandt Quirk Manor

410 South Fourth Street, Watertown, WI 53094
414-261-7917

Hosts: Wayne and Elda Zuleger

*T*his Greek revival home, constructed by Frederick Brandt, has been restored to its 1875 elegance. The manor features Ionic pillars inside and out, stained glass windows, marble sinks, marble and ceramic fireplaces, parquet flooring, and decorative plaster accents. Guests are welcome to relax in the grandeur of this bygone era.

The manor has five guest rooms, three with adjoining sitting areas. Three have private baths and two share a bath. The manor is furnished with many period antiques.

Come, relax. Enjoy our hospitality, tour the Octagon House and First Kindergarten. Walk the riverfront boardwalk, swim at the aquatic center, or view many of the historic homes on one of four walking tours of the city.

Rates at the Brandt Quirk Manor range from $55–$75.
Rates include a full breakfast.

Crescent Cheesecake

This will tantalize your taste buds. It's easy to make, yet delicious, and can easily be cut in half.

serves 24

2   cans Pillsbury crescent rolls
2   8-ounce packages cream cheese
1½   cups sugar, divided
1   egg, separated
1   teaspoon cinnamon
½   cup pecans or walnuts

Spread 1 can crescent rolls in a greased 9x13-inch cake pan. Beat cream cheese, 1 cup sugar, and egg yolk; spread mixture over unbaked crescent rolls. Spread second can of crescent rolls on top of mixture. Beat egg white and brush on top of crescent rolls. Combine remaining ½ cup sugar with cinnamon and nuts. Sprinkle over egg whites. Bake in 350-degree oven for 25-30 minutes.

Crystal River Bed & Breakfast

E1369 Rural Road, Waupaca, WI 54981
715-258-5333

Hosts: Gene and Lois Sorenson

reshly ironed sheets, down comforters, locally made candy, and a profusion of pillows all greet the guests as they enter their room. Located on the Crystal River just outside Waupaca in the National Register Historic District of Rural, chosen one of the nation's 200 most charming towns and villages, this unique 1853 home has much to offer. Featured in *Wisconsin Trails* magazine, chosen for the inside cover of the 1990 Wisconsin Tourism publication *Winter Adventures*, and featured as the front page article of *Milwaukee Sentinel* travel section, this bed and breakfast offers seven luxurious rooms, five with private baths, three with fireplaces and one with a private balcony overlooking the river. Our newest room has a double heart-shaped whirlpool. The Crystal River Bed & Breakfast is truly a luxurious step back in time.

Central Wisconsin is fast becoming the mecca of antique shop lovers. That, as well as the 23 spring-fed Chain-O-Lakes, Rustic Roads, Hartman Creek State Park, and unique gift shops make the Waupaca area "the place to visit."

Rates at the Crystal River Bed & Breakfast range from $55–$95.
Rates include a full breakfast.

Super Duper French Toast

This recipe was taken from Mature *magazine and slightly changed. It is easy to make and gives a tangy flavor to the French toast.*

serves 4

1	teaspoon finely grated orange peel
1	cup orange juice
1/3	cup milk
6	eggs
3	tablespoons sugar
1/4	teaspoon vanilla extract
1/4	teaspoon salt
8	3/4-inch-thick slices bread
	Powdered sugar

The night before serving, combine orange peel, orange juice, milk, eggs, sugar, vanilla, and salt; mix well. Dip bread into mixture and place on a 10x16-inch pan. Pour excess mixture over bread. Cover and refrigerate overnight.

Heat griddle to 325 degrees and fry bread until brown, approximately 8 minutes. Sprinkle with powdered sugar, cut and serve with or without meat.

The Rose Ivy Inn

228 South Watertown Street, Waupun, WI 53963-2140
414-324-2127

Hosts: Melody and Ken Kris

Guest comfort and attention to detail are priorities at the Rose Ivy Inn. Each of the beautifully appointed bedrooms reflects the Victorian charm innkeepers Melody and Ken enjoy sharing with their guests.

Celebrate the beginning of each day with a delicious breakfast served in the elegant dining room or, on warm mornings, in the glass-enclosed sun porch.

Enjoy nearby Horicon Marsh Wildlife Refuge where walking the trails and birding are favorite past-times. Borrow the Inn's bicycles and ride the Wild Goose Bike Trail, which offers 34 miles of great biking, cross-country skiing, or hiking. Leisurely stroll the streets of historic Waupun or curl up with one of the many great books from the Rose Ivy Inn library.

The Rose Ivy Inn, an elegant Queen-Anne bed and breakfast, is the perfect place for that special holiday you deserve to take.

Innkeepers Melody and Ken invite you to come and enjoy the beauty and warmth of their lovely, historic inn.

Rates at the Rose Ivy Inn range from $80-$90.
Rates include a full breakfast.

Rose Ivy Inn Breakfast Bread Pudding with Raspberry Sauce

Our guests agree that, with this dish and our other delicious breakfast specialties, we have created a memorable way to start their day.

serves 6-8

8	cups French bread cubes		Raspberry Sauce:
6	large eggs	2	16-ounce packages frozen raspberries in syrup, thawed
1/2	cup sugar		
2	teaspoons vanilla extract		
1	teaspoon cinnamon	1 1/4	cups water
1/4	teaspoon nutmeg	3	tablespoons cornstarch
1/8	teaspoon salt	3	tablespoons lemon juice, freshly squeezed
1/4	cup melted butter		
2	cups milk	1	tablespoon Chambord
1	cup whipping cream or half-and-half	1/4	cup white wine
		1/4	cup sugar

Grease a 9x13-inch glass pan. Spread bread cubes in pan. Combine remaining bread pudding ingredients in a 2-quart bowl and mix well. Gently pour over bread cubes to saturate. Cover and refrigerate overnight.

The next morning, remove cover and bake at 350 degrees for 30 minutes. Reduce temperature to 250 degrees. Cover bread pudding lightly with aluminum foil, and bake 40 minutes longer.

Puree raspberries in a blender. Strain raspberries through a fine sieve to remove seeds. Combine remaining ingredients in a 2-quart saucepan. Add raspberry puree. Cook over medium heat until thickened, stirring constantly. Serve over hot bread pudding.

Victoria-On-Main Bed & Breakfast

622 West Main Street, Whitewater, WI 53190
414-473-8400

Hostess: Nancy Wendt

Step back into an era of Victorian graciousness and relax in this stately 1895 Queen Anne home. Enjoy lovely rooms with ample space to stretch out and read in a comfortable antique chair. Delight in the artisanship of exquisite woodwork and romantic lace curtains. Rest comfortably with down pillows and comforters and fine cotton sheets dried in the fresh air. Awake to the aroma of fresh coffee and be served a tempting full breakfast. A smoke-free environment is provided, and a guest kitchen is available for your use.

Enjoy biking, hiking, swimming, boating, and cross-country skiing in the Kettle Moraine area. The bed and breakfast is located adjacent to University of Wisconsin-Whitewater and its various cultural and sporting events.

Have a relaxing stay at Victoria-On-Main, and leave with pleasant memories.

Rates at the Victoria-On-Main Bed & Breakfast range from $48–$75.
Rates include a full breakfast.

Banana Split Bread

This is a great snack upon arrival. I double the recipe and use the small loaf pans. I try to freeze a couple of loaves, but they usually get eaten before they get to the freezer!

makes 1 large or 2 small loaves

1/2	cup butter, softened	2	cups flour
1	cup sugar	1	teaspoon baking powder
1	large egg	1/2	teaspoon baking soda
1	cup ripe bananas, mashed, about 2 large bananas	3/4	teaspoon salt
		1	cup semi-sweet chocolate chips
3	tablespoons milk	1/2	cup chopped pecans

In large mixing bowl, cream butter, sugar, and egg with an electric mixer. Beat until fluffy, about 3 minutes. Set aside.

In small bowl, mix bananas and milk. Set aside. Sift together flour, baking powder, baking soda, and salt.

Alternately add dry ingredients and banana mixture to creamed butter mixture, stirring after each addition with rubber spatula until dry ingredients are blended. Stir in chocolate chips and pecans.

Spoon into one 9x5-inch or two $7^1/_2$ x $3^1/_2$-inch loaf pans that have been greased and floured. Bake 50-60 minutes in 350-degree oven. Cool in pan on wire rack 10 minutes before removing. Finish cooling on wire rack.

Birdsong Bed & Breakfast

930 East County A, P.O. Box 391, Wild Rose, WI 54984-0391
414-622-3770

Hosts: Walt and Sallyann Bouwens

Birdsong Bed & Breakfast is a quiet village home ready to welcome guests to spacious rooms and personal comforts. An extensive library offers books on a great variety of subjects, and art pieces collected during international travels are integral components to the decor. In the summer, a 70-foot screened-in veranda furnished with white wicker furniture is a refreshing oasis from the sun and heat. In winter, a blazing fire in the library fireplace beckons guests to relax, and who cares if it snows all night? Note: few people need lunch after our full breakfast.

Rates at the Birdsong Bed & Breakfast range from $65–$75.
Rates include a full breakfast.

Overnight Warm Fruit Compote

*I at least double the recipe! Easy to make the night before,
I plug it in just before I go to bed. The scent of cardamom is
wonderful to wake up with!*

serves 8

1	29-ounce can pear halves
1	29-ounce can peach slices
1	pound dried apricots, halved
1/2	cup light brown sugar, firmly packed
2	tablespoons butter
2	6-ounce cans pineapple juice
1/2	teaspoon ground cardamom
1/4	cup slivered almonds
1	cup heavy cream
	Nutmeg

Drain pear halves and peach slices. Quarter pears. Place apricots in bottom of electric slow-cooker; arrange pears and peaches over apricots. Sprinkle brown sugar evenly over fruit. Dot with butter. Pour pineapple juice over mixture and sprinkle with cardamom. Cover and cook on low heat overnight, approximately 8 hours.

Just before serving, sprinkle nuts on fruit and whip the cream until soft peaks form. Serve compote warm, accompanied by whipped cream dusted with nutmeg.

Historic Bennett House

825 Oak Street, Wisconsin Dells, WI 53965
608-254-2500

Hosts: Rich and Gail Obermeyer

The Obermeyers host guests year-round in this 1863 adult retreat, located one block from downtown shops, boats, ducks, and river scenery. A full breakfast is served every morning. On weekends, guests enjoy Rich's mini-lectures on H. H. Bennett, pioneer nature photographer of the Dells, whose work is on display at the Smithsonian.

Our home is on the National Register of Historic Places. Two guest rooms upstairs share a bedroom-size bath with an original claw foot tub and lots of bubble bath. This bath also includes hand-painted Italian sinks. The third guest room includes a large sitting room and private bath on the main floor. The home is warm, casually elegant, with many collectibles—a true European-style retreat.

Rates at the Historic Bennett House range from $70–$90.
Rates include a full breakfast.

Midmorning Delight
(A Richard Original)

This is very easy to prepare. Richard especially likes the combination of hot and cold together.

serves 2

1   English muffin
      Mayonnaise
2   slices deli ham
      Course ground mustard with horseradish
2   slices medium cheddar cheese
2   slices tomato
      Sour cream
      Fresh parsley tips

Separate English muffin with a fork and toast. Spread each half with mayonnaise and top each with a ham slice. Spread with mustard and top with cheese.

Place on a cookie sheet and bake in a 400-degree oven until the cheese melts, about 5 minutes. Add a tomato slice and a dollop of cold sour cream to each half. Garnish with parsley tips.

The Nash House–A Bed & Breakfast

1020 Oak Street, Wisconsin Rapids, WI 54494
715-424-2001

Hosts: Phyllis and Jim Custer

The Nash House, built in 1903, offers three bedrooms for your relaxation and comfort. Queen-size beds, family antiques, beautiful quilts, and private baths are waiting for you. The rooms are named for the three Nash children: Jean, Tom, and Philleo.

We have a casual and relaxed atmosphere, love to kick off our shoes, sit on the sofa, and visit with our guests over a cup of tea, coffee, or a glass of wine.

The Wisconsin Rapids area includes outdoor activities as well as excellent dining, casino gambling, and historical and industrial places to see. Business travelers are very welcome.

Come and enjoy!

*Rates at The Nash House are $40 and $50 for single
and $10 for each additional person.
Rates include a full breakfast.*

Chocolate Freezer Goodies

*These are small, light and have
just the right amount of sweetness to top off breakfast.
Guests enjoy the novelty of dessert at breakfast time.
The goodies also make a nice treat just before bed.*

makes 15-20

1	cup butter
2	cups powdered sugar
4	1-ounce squares unsweetened chocolate
4	eggs
2	teaspoons vanilla extract
1/2	cup chopped nuts, optional
20	vanilla wafers

In large mixing bowl, cream butter and powdered sugar. Melt chocolate and add to butter and sugar. Beat in eggs, one at a time, until frothy. Add vanilla and nuts.

Crush vanilla wafers into crumbs. Place small amount of crumbs in bottom of each cup of a mini-muffin tin. Fill each cup with chocolate mixture and top with a sprinkle of crumbs, pressing them lightly into tops.

Place muffin tin in freezer. Remove 10 minutes before serving.

Index of Recipes

1997 WBBA Members

Bold type: For more information on this Inn, see the page listed

CITY	INN/PHONE

Albany   Albany Guest House   608-862-3636
   Banana Whole Grain Waffles, page 6
  Oak Hill Manor Bed & Breakfast   608-862-1400
   Eggs Florentine, page 8
  Sugar River Inn Bed & Breakfast   608-862-1248

Algoma   Amberwood Inn   414-487-3471

Allenton   Addison House   414-629-9993

Alma   The Gallery House   608-685-4975

Appleton   Franklin Street Inn   414-739-3702
  The Queen Anne Bed & Breakfast   414-739-7966

Ashland   The Residenz   715-682-2425

Baileys Harbor   The Blacksmith Inn   414-839-9222
  The Potter's Door Inn Bed & Breakfast   414-839-2003

Baraboo   Frantiques Showplace   608-356-5273
  Pinehaven Bed & Breakfast   608-356-3489
   Blueberry Coffee Cake, page 10
  The Victorian Rose   608-356-7828

Barnes   Sunset Resort Bed & Breakfast Lodge   715-795-2449
   Pannekuechen (Dutch), page 12

Bayfield   Apple Tree Inn   715-779-5572
  The Artesian House   715-779-3338
  Baywood Place Bed & Breakfast   715-779-3690
  Cooper Hill House Bed & Breakfast   715-779-5060
  Morning Glory Bed & Breakfast   715-779-5621
  The Old Rittenhouse Inn   715-779-5111
   Wild Rice Pancakes, page 14
  Pinehurst Inn at Pike's Creek   715-779-3676
  Thimbleberry Inn Bed & Breakfast   715-779-5757
   Craisin Yogurt Muffins, page 16

Beaver Dam   The Victorian Bed & Breakfast   414-885-9601

Belleville   Cameo Rose Bed & Breakfast   608-424-6340

Black Creek   Old Coach Inn Bed & Breakfast   414-984-3840

Brodhead   Buckskin Lodge Bed & Breakfast   608-897-2914

Browntown   Four Seasons   608-966-1680
  Old School Inn Bed & Breakfast   608-966-1848

Burlington   Hillcrest Inn & Carriage House   414-763-4706
   Karen's Quick and Easy Blueberry Muffins, page 18
  Idle Acres Inn Bed & Breakfast   414-539-2229

Cable   Connors Bed & Breakfast   800-848-3932

Cambridge/Rockdale   Cambridge House Bed & Breakfast   608-423-7008
  The Night Heron Bed, Books & Breakfast   608-423-4141

Camp Douglas   Sunnyfield Farm Bed & Breakfast   608-427-3686

Campbellsport   Mielke-Mauk House   414-533-8602
  Newcastle Pines   414-533-5252

Cascade   Timberlake Inn   414-528-8481

Cashton   Cannondalen   800-947-6261

Cassville   The Geiger House   608-725-5419
  River View Bed & Breakfast   608-725-5895

Cedarburg   Stagecoach Inn   414-375-0208
   Apple-Cinnamon French Toast, page 20

Chetek   The Annandale Inn   715-837-1974
  Trail's End Bed & Breakfast   715-924-2641
   Cinnamon Coffee Cake, page 22

CITY	INN/PHONE
Chippewa Falls	McGilvray's Victorian Bed & Breakfast 715-720-1600
	Pleasant View Bed & Breakfast 715-382-4401
Cochrane	The Rosewood Bed & Breakfast 608-248-2940
Columbus	Dering House 414-623-2015
	Maple Leaf Inn Bed & Breakfast 414-623-5166
Cornucopia	The Village Inn 715-742-3941
Crandon	**Courthouse Square Bed & Breakfast 715-478-2549**
	Orange Raisin Scones with Orange Butter, page 24
Cross Plains	Enchanted Valley Bed & Breakfast 608-798-4554
	The Past & Present Inn 608-798-4441
	Apple Filled Oven French Toast, page 26
Cumberland	The Rectory Bed & Breakfast 715-822-3151
Delavan	**The Allyn Mansion Inn, Ltd. 414-728-9090**
	Allyn Mansion Fried Apples, page 28
	Lakeside Manor Inn 414-728-5354
De Pere	**Birch Creek Inn 414-336-7575**
	K-Bars, page 30
	R & R Homestead 414-336-8244
Durand	Ryan House Bed & Breakfast 715-672-8563
Eagle	Eagle Centre House 414-363-4700
Eagle River	The Bed & Breakfast at Hilltop House 715-479-2248
	Brennan Manor Bed & Breakfast 715-479-7353
	English Breakfast Scones, page 32
	The Inn at Pinewood 715-479-4114
	Baked Apple Pancake, page 34
East Troy	Mitten Farm 414-642-5530
	Pine Ridge 414-594-3269
Eau Claire	The Atrium Bed & Breakfast 715-833-9045
	Otter Creek Inn 715-832-2945
Edgerton	**The Olde Parsonage Bed & Breakfast 608-884-6490**
	Zucchini Bread, page 36
Elkhorn	**Ye Olde Manor House Bed & Breakfast 414-742-2450**
	"Never Fail" Cheese Souffle, page 38
Ellison Bay	Country Woods Bed & Breakfast 414-854-5706
Elroy	East View Bed & Breakfast 608-463-7564
	Stillested Bed & Breakfast 800-462-4980
	Waarvik's Century Farm B & B 608-462-8595
Endeavor	**Neenah Creek Inn & Pottery 608-587-2229**
	Grilled Chicken Kabobs, page 40
Ephraim	Eagle Harbor Inn 414-854-2121
	The Ephraim Inn 414-854-4515
	The French Country Inn of Ephraim 414-854-4001
	Dates & Millet, page 42
	Prairie Garden Bed & Breakfast of Door County 414-854-2555
Evansville	Holmes Victorian Inn 608-882-6866
Fennimore	The Gazebo Bed & Breakfast 608-822-3928
Ferryville	Mississippi Humble Bush 608-737-3022
Fish Creek	**The Birchwood Bed & Breakfast 414-868-3214**
	Irish Soda Bread, page 44
	The Juniper Inn 414-839-2629
	Thorp House Inn & Cottages 414-868-2444
	The Whistling Swan Inn 414-868-3442
	Door County Cherry
	Sour Cream Coffee Cake, page 46
	The White Gull Inn 414-868-3517
	Cherry Stuffed French Toast, page 48
Florence	Lakeside Bed & Breakfast 715-528-3259
	Fruit Delight, page 50

CITY	INN/PHONE
Fontana	Strawberry Hill Bed & Breakfast 414-275-5998
Fort Atkinson	La Grange Bed & Breakfast 414-563-1421
	Lamp Post Inn 414-563-6561
	Sorbet, page 52
Frederic	Gandy Dancer Bed & Breakfast 715-327-8750
Genoa City	House on the Hill Bed & Breakfast 414-279-6466
Gills Rock	Harbor House Inn 414-854-5196
Glen Haven	Parson's Inn Bed & Breakfast 608-794-2491
Grand View	Hummingbird Bed & Breakfast 715-763-3214
Green Bay	The Astor House 414-432-3585
Green Lake	**McConnell Inn 414-294-6430**
	Apple Cheese Pancakes, page 54
Hammond	**Summit Farm Bed & Breakfast 715-796-2617**
	Crab Apple Liqueur, page 56
Hancock	Walker House Bed & Breakfast 414-763-2615
Hartford	Jordan House Bed & Breakfast 414-673-5643
Hayward	**Edgewater Inn Bed & Breakfast 715-462-9412**
	Oatmeal Pudding, page 58
	Lumberman's Mansion Inn 715-634-3012
	Crispy Cookie Coffee Cake, page 60
	Mustard Seed Bed & Breakfast 715-634-2908
	Breakfast Burritos, page 62
	Spider Lake Lodge Bed & Breakfast 800-OLD-WISC
Hazel Green	Wisconsin House Stage Coach Inn 608-854-2233
Hazelhurst	Hazelhurst Inn 715-356-6571
Hillsboro	Edgecombe Inn 608-489-2915
	Tiger Inn 608-489-2918
Hollandale	Old Granary Inn 608-967-2140
Hudson	Grapevine Inn Bed & Breakfast 715-386-1989
	Jefferson-Day House 715-386-7111
	Oven Omelette, page 64
	Phipps Inn 715-386-0800
	Cranberry Muffins
	with Hot Buttered Rum Sauce, page 66
Iola	**Iris Inn 715-445-4848**
	Orange Cranberry Muffins, page 68
	Taylor House 715-445-2204
Iron River	Iron River Trout Haus 715-372-4219
Janesville	Antique Rose Bed & Breakfast 608-754-8180
Juneau	**Country Retreat on Primrose Lane 414-386-2912**
	Streusel Coffee Cake, page 70
Kendall	Cabin at Trails End 608-427-3877
Kewaskum	Country Ridge Inn Bed & Breakfast 414-626-4853
	The Doctors Inn Bed & Breakfast 414-626-2666
Kewaunee	Chelsea Rose Bed & Breakfast 414-388-2012
	Duvall House 414-388-0501
	The "Gables" 414-388-0220
	Historic Norman General Store 414-388-4580
	The Kewaunee House 414-388-1017
La Crosse	The Martindale House Bed & Breakfast 608-782-4224
La Farge	**Trillium 608-625-4492**
	Scottish Raspberry Buns, page 72
Lac Du Flambeau	Ty-Bach 715-588-7851
Lake Delton	**The Swallow's Nest Bed & Breakfast 608-254-6900**
	Fluffy Cheese Omelet, page 74

CITY	INN/PHONE
Lake Geneva	General Boyd's Bed & Breakfast 414-248-3543
	Pederson Victorian Bed & Breakfast 414-248-9110
	Kristi's Breakfast Corn Bake, page 76
	Roses, A Bed & Breakfast 414-248-4344
Lake Mills	**The Fargo Mansion Inn 414-648-3654**
	Cheese Strata, page 78
Lancaster	Maple Harris Guest House 608-723-4717
	Martha's Bed & Breakfast 608-723-4711
Lodi	Prairie Garden Bed & Breakfast 608-592-5187
	Victorian Treasure Bed & Breakfast Inn 800-859-5199
	Kimberly's Strawberry Coffee Cake, page 80
Lomira	The White Shutters 414-269-4056
Luxemburg	Bit of the Bay 414-866-9901
Madison	Annie's Bed & Breakfast 608-244-2224
	Arbor House, An Environmental Inn 608-238-2981
	Canterbury Inn 608-258-8899
	Collins House Bed & Breakfast 608-255-4230
	Mansion Hill Inn 800-798-9070
	Stoney Oaks 608-278-1646
	University Heights Bed & Breakfast 608-233-3340
Maiden Rock	**Harrisburg Inn Bed & Breakfast 715-448-4500**
	Sausage Gravy Harrisburg Style, page 82
	Pine Creek Lodge 715-448-3203
Manawa	Ferg Haus Inn 414-596-2946
Manitowish Waters	Friar's Tuckaway Bed & Breakfast 715-543-8231
Manitowoc	**Arbor Manor Bed & Breakfast 414-684-6095**
	Spiced Apples, page 84
	The Jarvis House Bed & Breakfast 414-682-2103
	Morning Glorious Muffins, page 86
Marinette	M & M Victorian Inn 715-732-9531
Mayville	J & R's Sherm Inn 414-387-4642
Mazomanie	Quiet Woods Bed & Breakfast 608-795-4954
Menomonee Falls	**Hitching Post Bed & Breakfast 414-255-1496**
	Syl's Scratzkis, page 88
Menomonie	**Cedar Trail Guesthouse 715-664-8828**
	Cedar Trail's Kidney Bean Cookies, page 90
Mequon	American Country Farm Bed
	& Breakfast Guest House 414-242-0194
Merrill	**The Brick House Bed & Breakfast 715-536-3230**
	Norwegian Kringler, page 92
	Candlewick Inn 800-382-4376
Middleton	**The Middleton Beach Inn 608-831-6446**
	Broccoli Cheese Strata, page 94
Milton	Chase on the Hill 608-868-6646
Mineral Point	The Cothren House 608-987-2612
	The House of the Brau-Meister 608-987-2913
	Knudson's Guest House 608-987-2733
	Wilson House Inn 608-987-3600
Minocqua	Kinsale Bed & Breakfast 715-356-3296
	The Minocqua Inn 715-358-2578
	Whitehaven Bed & Breakfast 715-356-9097
Monroe	**Victorian Garden Bed & Breakfast 608-328-1720**
	Sun-dried Tomato/Cheese Frittata, page 96
Montreal	**The Inn Bed & Breakfast 715-561-5180**
	Honey Buns, page 98

CITY	INN/PHONE
Mountain	Winter Green 715-276-6885
New Glarus	Country House Inn 608-527-5399
	Jeanne-Marie's Bed & Breakfast 608-527-5059
	Linden Inn & Simple Gifts Gallery 608-527-2675
	Spring Valley Creek Bed & Breakfast 608-527-2314
	Zentner Haus 608-527-2121
Ogema	**Timm's Hill Bed & Breakfast 715-767-5288**
	Timm's Hill Quiche, page 100
Onalaska	Lumber Baron Inn 608-781-8938
Osceola	**Pleasant Lake Inn Bed & Breakfast 800-294-2545**
	Honey Puffed Pancake, page 102
	St. Croix River Inn 715-294-4248
Pardeeville	The Country Rose Bed & Breakfast 608-429-2035
	Gator Gully Bed & Breakfast 608-429-2754
Pepin	**A Summer Place 715-442-2132**
	Bananas Exceptional, page 104
Phelps	The Hazen Inn 715-545-3600
	The Limberlost Inn 715-545-2685
Phillips	East Highland Bed & Breakfast 715-339-3492
Plain	Bettinger House Bed & Breakfast 608-546-2951
	The Kraemer House Bed & Breakfast 608-546-3161
	Raspberry Coffee Cake, page 106
Plainfield	**Johnson Inn 715-335-4383**
	Apple Glazed Sausages, page 108
Platteville	Cunningham House Bed & Breakfast 608-348-5532
	The Gribble House Bed & Breakfast 608-348-7282
	Walnut Ridge 608-348-9359
Plymouth	B.L. Nutt Inn 414-892-8566
	Beverly's Log Guest House 414-892-6064
	Hillwind Farm Bed & Breakfast 414-892-2199
	Spring Farm Cottage 414-892-2101
	Yankee Hill Inn Bed & Breakfast 414-892-2222
	Applesauce Oatmeal Muffins, page 110
Port Washington	The Grand Inn 414-284-6719
	The Inn at Old Twelve Hundred 414-268-1200
	Port Washington Inn 414-284-5583
	Strawberry Stuffed French Toast, page 112
Portage	**Breese Waye Bed & Breakfast 608-742-5281**
	Breakfast Banana Split, page 114
	Riverbend Inn 800-820-8264
Poynette	**Jamieson House Inn 608-635-4100**
	Devonshire Cream, page 116
Prairie Du Chien	Neumann House Bed & Breakfast 608-326-8104
Prairie Du Sac	The Graff House Bed & Breakfast 608-643-6978
Prescott	The Arbor Inn 715-262-4522
Princeton	Ellison's Gray Lion Inn 414-295-4101
Racine	College Avenue Bed & Breakfast 414-637-7870
	Linen & Lace Bed & Breakfast 414-534-4966
	Mansards On-the-Lake 414-632-1135
Reedsburg	**Parkview Bed & Breakfast 608-524-4333**
	Large Breakfast Pancake, page 118
Richland Center	**Lamb's Inn Bed & Breakfast 608-585-4301**
	Italian Vegetable Quiche, page 120
River Falls	**Knollwood House Bed & Breakfast 800-435-0628**
	Rhubarb Muffins, page 122
Saint Germain	St. Germain Bed & Breakfast 715-479-8007
Shawano	The Prince Edward 715-526-2805

CITY	INN/PHONE
Sheboygan	Brownstone Inn 414-451-0644
	The Scheele House 414-458-0998
Sheboygan Falls	Rochester Inn 414-467-3123
Shell Lake	Maple Syrup Ranch Bed & Breakfast 715-468-2251
Sister Bay	Hidden Gardens Bed & Breakfast 414-854-5487
	The Inn on Maple 414-854-5107
	The Wooden Heart Inn 414-854-9097
	Stuffed French Toast with Blueberry Sauce, page 124
Sparta	The Franklin Victorian Bed & Breakfast 800-845-8767
	Just-N-Trails Bed & Breakfast 800-488-4521
	Cranberry Coffee Cake, page 126
	Strawberry Lace Inn 608-269-7878
Spooner	Green Valley Inn 715-635-7300
Spread Eagle	**The Lodge at River's Edge 715-696-3406**
	Divine Buttermilk Hot Cakes with Orange Syrup, page 128
Spring Green	Deer Acres 608-588-7299
	Hill Street Bed & Breakfast 608-588-7751
	Cappuccino Chip Muffins, page 130
Springbrook	The Stout Trout 715-466-2790
Stevens Point	The Birdhouse 715-341-0084
	Dreams of Yesteryear Bed & Breakfast 715-341-4525
	Dutch Apple Roll, page 132
	Marcyanna's Bed & Breakfast 715-341-9922
	Victorian Swan on Water 715-345-0595
	Fabulous Noodle Kugel, page 134
Stockholm	Hyggelig Hus 715-442-2086
Stone Lake	The Lake House Bed & Breakfast and Art Gallery 715-865-6803
	New Mountain Bed & Breakfast 800-NEW-MT-BB
Sturgeon Bay	Chanticleer Guest House 414-746-0334
	Colonial Gardens Bed & Breakfast 414-746-9192
	The Gray Goose Bed & Breakfast 414-743-9100
	Zucchini-Tomato Pie, page 136
	Hearthside Bed & Breakfast Inn 414-746-2136
	Popovers, page 138
	Inn at Cedar Crossing 414-743-4200
	Dried Cherry and Almond Scones, page 140
	Inn The Pines 414-743-9319
	Quiet Cottage 414-743-4526
	The Scofield House Bed & Breakfast 414-743-7727
	Bacon-Cheddar Baked Eggs, page 142
	Van Clay Guest House 414-743-6611
	White Lace Inn 414-743-1105
	Bonnie's Lemon Blueberry Muffins, page 144
	Whitefish Bay Farm Bed & Breakfast 414-743-1560
Superior	Crawford House Bed & Breakfast 715-394-5271
Tomahawk	Swan Song Bed & Breakfast 715-453-1173
Two Rivers	**Red Forest Bed & Breakfast 414-793-1794**
	Maple Bran Muffins, page 146
Verona	Beat Road Farm Bed & Breakfast 608-437-6500
Viroqua	Viroqua Heritage Inn 608-637-3306
Washington Island	Island House Bed & Breakfast 414-847-2779
Waterford	River View Inn 414-534-5049
Waterloo	Carousel B & B 414-478-2536
Watertown	**Brandt Quirk Manor 414-261-7917**
	Crescent Cheesecake, page 148
	Karlshuegel Inn 414-261-3980
Waukesha	Mill Creek Farm Bed & Breakfast 414-542-4311

CITY	INN/PHONE
Waupaca	**Crystal River Bed & Breakfast 715-258-5333**
	Super Duper French Toast, page 150
	Green Fountain Inn 715-258-5171
	Thomas Pipe Inn 715-824-3161
	Walker's Barn Bed & Breakfast 800-870-0737
	White Horse Bed & Breakfast 715-258-6162
Waupun	**The Rose Ivy Inn 414-324-2127**
	Rose Ivy Breakfast Bread Pudding
	with Raspberry Sauce, page 152
Wausau	The Eliza Inn 715-842-2722
	Rosenberry Inn Bed & Breakfast 715-842-5733
Wauwatosa	The Little Red House Bed & Breakfast 414-479-0646
West Bend	Mayer-Pick Haus 414-335-1524
West Salem	Wolfway Farm 608-486-2686
Westby	Westby House 608-634-4112
Westfield	Martha's Ethnic Bed & Breakfast 608-296-3361
	Mill Pond Bed & Breakfast 608-296-1495
White Lake	Jesse's Historic Wolf River Lodge 715-882-2182
Whitehall	The Augustine House 715-538-4749
Whitewater	Hamilton House Bed & Breakfast 414-473-1900
	Victoria-on-Main Bed & Breakfast 414-473-8400
	Banana Split Bread, page 154
Wild Rose	**Birdsong Bed & Breakfast 414-622-3770**
	Overnight Warm Fruit Compote, page 156
Williams Bay	Bailey House 414-245-9149
Wilton	Rice's Whispering Pines 608-435-6531
Wisconsin Dells	Hawk's View Bed & Breakfast 608-254-2979
	Historic Bennett House 608-254-2500
	Midmorning Delight (A Richard Original), page 158
	Thunder Valley 608-254-4145
Wisconsin Rapids	**The Nash House—A Bed & Breakfast 715-424-2001**
	Chocolate Freezer Goodies, page 160
	Sigrid's Bed & Breakfast 715-423-3846
Woodruff	Jo's Place North Bed & Breakfast 715-356-6682

If you have enjoyed this book, you'll love other books and guides from Amherst Press. From food festivals and farmers' markets to fine restaurants, Books-To-Go from Amherst Press is your source for regional interest books, recreational destination guides, and fine cookbooks.

To order
Have Breakfast With Us...Again
or for a free catalog, call 800-333-8122.

Amherst Press
PO Box 296
318 N. Main Street
Amherst, Wisconsin 54406